DOVER · THRIFT · EDITIONS

Selected Poems

JOHN DONNE

DOVER PUBLICATIONS, INC.
New York

DOVER THRIFT EDITIONS

GENERAL EDITOR: STANLEY APPELBAUM
EDITOR OF THIS VOLUME: SHANE WELLER

Copyright

Copyright © 1993 by Dover Publications, Inc.
All rights reserved under Pan American and International Copyright Conventions.

Published in Canada by General Publishing Company, Ltd., 30 Lesmill Road, Don Mills, Toronto, Ontario.
Published in the United Kingdom by Constable and Company, Ltd., 3 The Lanchesters, 162–164 Fulham Palace Road, London W6 9ER.

Bibliographical Note

This Dover edition, first published in 1993, is a new selection of poems, reprinted from *John Donne: Complete Poetry and Selected Prose*, published by the Nonesuch Press, Bloomsbury, in 1929. The Note and the alphabetical lists of titles and first lines have been prepared specially for the present edition, in which the spelling of the texts has been modernized.

Library of Congress Cataloging-in-Publication Data

Donne, John, 1572–1631.
    [Poems. Selections]
    Selected poems / John Donne.
        p.   cm. — (Dover thrift editions)
    A new selection of poems, reprinted from Complete poetry and selected prose, published in 1929.
    Includes index.
    ISBN 0-486-27788-7 (pbk.)
    I. Title. II. Series.
PR2246.D67 1993
821'.3—dc20
                                                 93-21800
                                               CIP

Manufactured in the United States of America
Dover Publications, Inc., 31 East 2nd Street, Mineola, N.Y. 11501

Note

A learned and original master of paradox, John Donne (1572–1631) is now recognized as the foremost poet of the Jacobean age. From his early erotic and satiric verse to the later religious poetry, he displays what Coleridge has eloquently described as "Rhyme's sturdy cripple, fancy's maze and clue / Wit's forge and fire-blast, meaning's press and screw." His work, both the secular and the religious, is also one of the finest treatments in English literature of the themes of fidelity and betrayal, conviction and skepticism.

Most of Donne's greatest poetic achievements remained unpublished until after his death—although the two long *Anniversaries*, not included here, were published in 1611 and 1612—and there is still considerable uncertainty about the dates of composition of many of the poems, particularly the *Songs and Sonnets*, which some claim belong to the 1590s, others placing them in the first decade of the seventeenth century. Scholars have had somewhat more success dating the divine poems: *La Corona* and the first group of *Holy Sonnets* were most probably written between 1607 and 1609. Although the arrangement of the present selection is generic, not chronological, still it does give, in outline at least, some sense of Donne's poetic development.

In the present edition the spelling has been modernized.

Contents

Selected Poems

The Good Morrow

I wonder by my troth, what thou, and I
Did, till we loved? were we not weaned till then?
But sucked on country pleasures, childishly?
Or snorted we in the seven sleepers' den?
'Twas so; but this, all pleasures fancies be.
If ever any beauty I did see,
Which I desired, and got, 'twas but a dream of thee.

And now good morrow to our waking souls,
Which watch not one another out of fear;
For love, all love of other sights controls,
And makes one little room, an everywhere.
Let sea-discoverers to new worlds have gone,
Let maps to other, worlds on worlds have shown,
Let us possess one world, each hath one, and is one.

My face in thine eye, thine in mine appears,
And true plain hearts do in the faces rest,
Where can we find two better hemispheres
Without sharp north, without declining west?
Whatever dies, was not mixed equally;
If our two loves be one, or, thou and I
Love so alike, that none do slacken, none can die.

Song

Go, and catch a falling star,
    Get with child a mandrake root,
Tell me, where all past years are,
    Or who cleft the devil's foot,
Teach me to hear mermaids singing,
    Or to keep off envy's stinging,
            And find
            What wind
Serves to advance an honest mind.

1

If thou beest born to strange sights,
  Things invisible to see,
Ride ten thousand days and nights,
  Till age snow white hairs on thee,
Thou, when thou return'st, wilt tell me
All strange wonders that befell thee,
                And swear
                Nowhere
Lives a woman true, and fair.

If thou findst one, let me know,
  Such a pilgrimage were sweet;
Yet do not, I would not go,
  Though at next door we might meet,
Though she were true, when you met her,
And last, till you write your letter,
                Yet she
                Will be
False, ere I come, to two, or three.

Woman's Constancy

Now thou hast loved me one whole day,
Tomorrow when thou leav'st, what wilt thou say?
Wilt thou then antedate some new made vow?
                Or say that now
We are not just those persons, which we were?
Or, that oaths made in reverential fear
Of love, and his wrath, any may forswear?
Or, as true deaths, true marriages untie,
So lovers' contracts, images of those,
Bind but till sleep, death's image, them unloose?
                Or, your own end to justify,
For having purposed change, and falsehood, you
Can have no way but falsehood to be true?
Vain lunatic, against these 'scapes I could
                Dispute, and conquer, if I would,
                Which I abstain to do,
For by tomorrow, I may think so too.

The Undertaking

I have done one braver thing
　Than all the Worthies did,
And yet a braver thence doth spring,
　Which is, to keep that hid.

It were but madness now t'impart
　The skill of specular stone,
When he which can have learned the art
　To cut it, can find none.

So, if I now should utter this,
　Others (because no more
Such stuff to work upon, there is,)
　Would love but as before.

But he who loveliness within
　Hath found, all outward loathes,
For he who color loves, and skin,
　Loves but their oldest clothes.

If, as I have, you also do
　Virtue attired in woman see,
And dare love that, and say so too,
　And forget the he and she;

And if this love, though placed so,
　From profane men you hide,
Which will no faith on this bestow,
　Or, if they do, deride:

Then you have done a braver thing
　Than all the Worthies did;
And a braver thence will spring,
　Which is, to keep that hid.

The Sun Rising

        Busy old fool, unruly sun,
        Why dost thou thus,
Through windows, and through curtains call on us?
Must to thy motions lovers' seasons run?
        Saucy pedantic wretch, go chide
        Late schoolboys, and sour prentices,
   Go tell court-huntsmen, that the King will ride,
   Call country ants to harvest offices;
Love, all alike, no season knows, nor clime,
Nor hours, days, months, which are the rags of time.

        Thy beams, so reverend, and strong
        Why shouldst thou think?
I could eclipse and cloud them with a wink,
But that I would not lose her sight so long:
        If her eyes have not blinded thine,
        Look, and tomorrow late, tell me,
   Whether both the Indias of spice and mine
   Be where thou leftst them, or lie here with me.
Ask for those kings whom thou saw'st yesterday,
And thou shalt hear, all here in one bed lay.

        She is all states, and all princes, I,
        Nothing else is.
Princes do but play us; compared to this,
All honor's mimic; all wealth alchemy.
        Thou sun art half as happy as we,
        In that the world's contracted thus;
   Thine age asks ease, and since thy duties be
   To warm the world, that's done in warming us.
Shine here to us, and thou art everywhere;
This bed thy center is, these walls, thy sphere.

The Indifferent

I can love both fair and brown,
Her whom abundance melts, and her whom want betrays,
Her who loves loneness best, and her who masks and plays,
Her whom the country formed, and whom the town,
Her who believes, and her who tries,
Her who still weeps with spongy eyes,
And her who is dry cork, and never cries;
I can love her, and her, and you and you,
I can love any, so she be not true.

Will no other vice content you?
Will it not serve your turn to do, as did your mothers?
Or have you all old vices spent, and now would find out others?
Or doth a fear, that men are true, torment you?
Oh we are not, be not you so,
Let me, and do you, twenty know.
Rob me, but bind me not, and let me go.
Must I, who came to travel thorough you,
Grow your fixed subject, because you are true?

Venus heard me sigh this song,
And by love's sweetest part, variety, she swore,
She heard not this till now; and that it should be so no more.
She went, examined, and returned ere long,
And said, "Alas, some two or three
Poor heretics in love there be,
Which think to stablish dangerous constancy.
But I have told them, 'Since you will be true,
You shall be true to them, who are false to you.' "

The Canonization

For God's sake hold your tongue, and let me love,
    Or chide my palsy, or my gout,
My five gray hairs, or ruined fortune flout,
    With wealth your state, your mind with arts improve,

Take you a course, get you a place,
  Observe his Honor, or his Grace,
Or the King's real, or his stamped face
  Contemplate; what you will, approve,
  So you will let me love.

Alas, alas, who's injured by my love?
  What merchant's ships have my sighs drowned?
Who says my tears have overflowed his ground?
  When did my colds a forward spring remove?
    When did the heats which my veins fill
    Add one more to the plaguy bill?
Soldiers find wars, and lawyers find out still
  Litigious men, which quarrels move,
  Though she and I do love.

Call us what you will, we are made such by love;
  Call her one, me another fly,
We are tapers too, and at our own cost die,
  And we in us find the eagle and the dove.
    The phoenix riddle hath more wit
    By us; we two being one, are it.
So to one neutral thing both sexes fit,
  We die and rise the same, and prove
  Mysterious by this love.

We can die by it, if not live by love,
  And if unfit for tombs and hearse
Our legend be, it will be fit for verse;
  And if no piece of chronicle we prove,
    We'll build in sonnets pretty rooms;
    As well a well wrought urn becomes
The greatest ashes, as half-acre tombs,
  And by these hymns, all shall approve
  Us canonized for love.

And thus invoke us: "You whom reverend love
  Made one another's hermitage;
You, to whom love was peace, that now is rage;
  Who did the whole world's soul contract, and drove
    Into the glasses of your eyes
    (So made such mirrors, and such spies,

That they did all to you epitomize)
   Countries, towns, courts: beg from above
   A pattern of your love!"

The Triple Fool

   I am two fools, I know,
For loving, and for saying so
   In whining poetry;
But where's that wiseman, that would not be I,
   If she would not deny?
Then as th'earth's inward narrow crooked lanes
Do purge seawater's fretful salt away,
   I thought, if I could draw my pains
Through rhyme's vexation, I should them allay.
Grief brought to numbers cannot be so fierce,
For, he tames it, that fetters it in verse.

   But when I have done so,
Some man, his art and voice to show,
   Doth set and sing my pain,
And, by delighting many, frees again
   Grief, which verse did restrain.
To love and grief tribute of verse belongs,
But not of such as pleases when 'tis read,
   Both are increased by such songs:
For both their triumphs so are published,
And I, which was two fools, do so grow three;
Who are a little wise, the best fools be.

Song

Sweetest love, I do not go,
   For weariness of thee,
Nor in hope the world can show
   A fitter love for me;
     But since that I

Must die at last, 'tis best,
To use myself in jest
    Thus by feigned deaths to die.

Yesternight the sun went hence,
    And yet is here today,
He hath no desire nor sense,
    Nor half so short a way:
        Then fear not me,
But believe that I shall make
Speedier journeys, since I take
    More wings and spurs than he.

O how feeble is man's power,
    That if good fortune fall,
Cannot add another hour,
    Nor a lost hour recall!
        But come bad chance,
And we join to it our strength,
And we teach it art and length,
    Itself o'er us to advance.

When thou sigh'st, thou sigh'st not wind,
    But sigh'st my soul away,
When thou weep'st, unkindly kind,
    My life's blood doth decay.
        It cannot be
That thou lov'st me, as thou say'st,
If in thine my life thou waste,
    That art the best of me.

Let not thy divining heart
    Forethink me any ill,
Destiny may take thy part,
    And may thy fears fulfill;
        But think that we
Are but turned aside to sleep;
They who one another keep
    Alive, ne'er parted be.

The Legacy

When I died last, and, dear, I die
  As often as from thee I go,
  Though it be but an hour ago,
And lovers' hours be full eternity,
I can remember yet, that I
  Something did say, and something did bestow;
Though I be dead, which sent me, I should be
Mine own executor and legacy.

I heard me say, Tell her anon,
  That myself (that is you, not I)
  Did kill me, and when I felt me die,
I bid me send my heart, when I was gone,
But I alas could there find none,
  When I had ripped me, and searched where hearts did lie;
It killed me again, that I who still was true,
In life, in my last will should cozen you.

Yet I found something like a heart,
  But colors it, and corners had,
  It was not good, it was not bad,
It was entire to none, and few had part.
As good as could be made by art
  It seemed; and therefore for our losses sad,
I meant to send this heart instead of mine,
But oh, no man could hold it, for 'twas thine.

A Fever

Oh do not die, for I shall hate
  All women so, when thou art gone,
That thee I shall not celebrate,
  When I remember, thou wast one.

But yet thou canst not die, I know;
  To leave this world behind, is death,

But when thou from this world wilt go,
  The whole world vapors with thy breath.

Or if, when thou, the world's soul, goest,
  It stay, 'tis but thy carcass then,
The fairest woman, but thy ghost,
  But corrupt worms, the worthiest men.

O wrangling schools, that search what fire
  Shall burn this world, had none the wit
Unto this knowledge to aspire,
  That this her fever might be it?

And yet she cannot waste by this,
  Nor long bear this torturing wrong,
For such corruption needful is
  To fuel such a fever long.

These burning fits but meteors be,
  Whose matter in thee is soon spent.
Thy beauty, and all parts, which are thee,
  Are unchangeable firmament.

Yet 'twas of my mind, seizing thee,
  Though it in thee cannot persever.
For I had rather owner be
  Of thee one hour, than all else ever.

Air and Angels

Twice or thrice had I loved thee,
Before I knew thy face or name;
So in a voice, so in a shapeless flame,
Angels affect us oft, and worshiped be;
  Still when, to where thou wert, I came,
Some lovely glorious nothing I did see.
  But since my soul, whose child love is,
Takes limbs of flesh, and else could nothing do,
  More subtle than the parent is,
Love must not be, but take a body too,
  And therefore what thou wert, and who,

I bid love ask, and now
That it assume thy body, I allow,
And fix itself in thy lip, eye, and brow.

Whilst thus to ballast love, I thought,
And so more steadily to have gone,
With wares which would sink admiration,
I saw, I had love's pinnace overfraught,
    Every thy hair for love to work upon
Is much too much, some fitter must be sought;
    For, nor in nothing, nor in things
Extreme, and scatt'ring bright, can love inhere;
    Then as an angel, face and wings
Of air, not pure as it, yet pure doth wear,
    So thy love may be my love's sphere;
        Just such disparity
As is 'twixt air and angels' purity,
'Twixt women's love, and men's will ever be.

Break of Day

'Tis true, 'tis day; what though it be?
O wilt thou therefore rise from me?
Why should we rise, because 'tis light?
Did we lie down, because 'twas night?
Love which in spite of darkness brought us hither,
Should in despite of light keep us together.

Light hath no tongue, but is all eye;
If it could speak as well as spy,
This were the worst, that it could say,
That being well, I fain would stay,
And that I loved my heart and honor so,
That I would not from him, that had them, go.

Must business thee from hence remove?
Oh, that's the worst disease of love,

The poor, the foul, the false, love can
Admit, but not the busied man.
He which hath business, and makes love, doth do
Such wrong, as when a married man doth woo.

The Anniversary

   All kings, and all their favorites,
   All glory of honors, beauties, wits,
The sun itself, which makes times, as they pass,
Is elder by a year, now, than it was
When thou and I first one another saw:
All other things, to their destruction draw,
   Only our love hath no decay;
This, no tomorrow hath, nor yesterday,
Running it never runs from us away,
But truly keeps his first, last, everlasting day.

   Two graves must hide thine and my corse,
   If one might, death were no divorce.
Alas, as well as other princes, we
(Who prince enough in one another be)
Must leave at last in death, these eyes, and ears,
Oft fed with true oaths, and with sweet salt tears;
   But souls where nothing dwells but love
(All other thoughts being inmates) then shall prove
This, or a love increased there above,
When bodies to their graves, souls from their graves remove.

   And then we shall be throughly blessed,
   But we no more, than all the rest;
Here upon earth, we are kings, and none but we
Can be such kings, nor of such subjects be.
Who is so safe as we? where none can do
Treason to us, except one of us two.
   True and false fears let us refrain,
Let us love nobly, and live, and add again
Years and years unto years, till we attain
To write threescore: this is the second of our reign.

A Valediction: of My Name, in the Window

My name engraved herein,
Doth contribute my firmness to this glass,
   Which, ever since that charm, hath been
   As hard, as that which graved it, was;
Thine eye will give it price enough, to mock
     The diamonds of either rock.

   'Tis much that glass should be
As all confessing, and through-shine as I,
   'Tis more, that it shows thee to thee,
   And clear reflects thee to thine eye.
But all such rules, love's magic can undo,
     Here you see me, and I am you.

   As no one point, nor dash,
Which are but accessories to this name,
   The showers and tempests can outwash,
   So shall all times find me the same;
You this entireness better may fulfill,
     Who have the pattern with you still.

   Or if too hard and deep
This learning be, for a scratched name to teach,
   It, as a given death's-head keep,
   Lovers' mortality to preach,
Or think this ragged bony name to be
     My ruinous anatomy.

   Then, as all my souls be
Emparadised in you (in whom alone
   I understand, and grow and see),
   The rafters of my body, bone
Being still with you, the muscle, sinew, and vein,
     Which tile this house, will come again.

   Till my return, repair
And recompact my scattered body so.
   As all the virtuous powers which are
   Fixed in the stars, are said to flow

Into such characters, as graved be
    When these stars have supremacy:

So since this name was cut
When love and grief their exaltation had,
    No door 'gainst this name's influence shut;
    As much more loving, as more sad,
'Twill make thee; and thou shouldst, till I return,
    Since I die daily, daily mourn.

When thy inconsiderate hand
Flings ope this casement, with my trembling name,
    To look on one, whose wit or land,
    New battery to thy heart may frame,
Then think this name alive, and that thou thus
    In it offendst my genius.

And when thy melted maid,
Corrupted by thy lover's gold, and page,
    His letter at thy pillow hath laid,
    Disputed it, and tamed thy rage,
And thou begin'st to thaw towards him, for this,
    May my name step in, and hide his.

And if this treason go
To an overt act, and that thou write again;
    In superscribing, this name flow
    Into thy fancy, from the pane.
So, in forgetting thou rememberest right,
    And unaware to me shalt write.

But glass, and lines must be
No means our firm substantial love to keep;
    Near death inflicts this lethargy,
    And this I murmur in my sleep;
Impute this idle talk, to that I go,
    For dying men talk often so.

Twickenham Garden

Blasted with sighs, and surrounded with tears,
  Hither I come to seek the spring,
  And at mine eyes, and at mine ears,
Receive such balms, as else cure everything;
  But O, self-traitor, I do bring
The spider love, which transubstantiates all,
  And can convert manna to gall,
And that this place may thoroughly be thought
  True paradise, I have the serpent brought.

'Twere wholesomer for me, that winter did
  Benight the glory of this place,
  And that a grave frost did forbid
These trees to laugh, and mock me to my face;
  But that I may not this disgrace
Endure, nor yet leave loving, Love, let me
  Some senseless piece of this place be;
Make me a mandrake, so I may groan here,
  Or a stone fountain weeping out my year.

Hither with crystal vials, lovers come,
  And take my tears, which are love's wine,
  And try your mistress' tears at home,
For all are false, that taste not just like mine;
  Alas, hearts do not in eyes shine,
Nor can you more judge woman's thoughts by tears,
  Than by her shadow, what she wears.
O perverse sex, where none is true but she,
  Who's therefore true, because her truth kills me.

A Valediction: of Weeping

      Let me pour forth
My tears before thy face, whilst I stay here,
For thy face coins them, and thy stamp they bear,
And by this mintage they are something worth,

        For thus they be
        Pregnant of thee;
Fruits of much grief they are, emblems of more,
When a tear falls, that thou falls which it bore,
So thou and I are nothing then, when on a divers shore.

        On a round ball
A workman that hath copies by, can lay
An Europe, Afric, and an Asia,
And quickly make that, which was nothing, all,
        So doth each tear,
        Which thee doth wear,
A globe, yea world by that impression grow,
Till thy tears mixed with mine do overflow
This world, by waters sent from thee, my heaven dissolved so.

        O more than moon,
Draw not up seas to drown me in thy sphere,
Weep me not dead, in thine arms, but forbear
To teach the sea, what it may do too soon;
        Let not the wind
        Example find,
To do me more harm, than it purposeth;
Since thou and I sigh one another's breath,
Whoe'er sighs most, is cruelest, and hastes the other's death.

The Flea

Mark but this flea, and mark in this,
How little that which thou deny'st me is;
It sucked me first, and now sucks thee,
And in this flea, our two bloods mingled be;
Thou know'st that this cannot be said
A sin, nor shame, nor loss of maidenhead,
    Yet this enjoys before it woo,
    And pampered swells with one blood made of two,
    And this, alas, is more than we would do.

Oh stay, three lives in one flea spare,
Where we almost, yea more than married are.

This flea is you and I, and this
Our marriage bed, and marriage temple is;
Though parents grudge, and you, we are met,
And cloistered in these living walls of jet.
    Though use make you apt to kill me,
    Let not to that, self-murder added be,
    And sacrilege, three sins in killing three.

Cruel and sudden, hast thou since
Purpled thy nail, in blood of innocence?
Wherein could this flea guilty be,
Except in that drop which it sucked from thee?
Yet thou triumph'st, and say'st that thou
Find'st not thyself, nor me the weaker now;
    'Tis true, then learn how false fears be;
    Just so much honor, when thou yield'st to me,
    Will waste, as this flea's death took life from thee.

The Curse

Whoever guesses, thinks, or dreams he knows
Who is my mistress, wither by this curse;
        His only, and only his purse
        May some dull heart to love dispose,
And she yield then to all that are his foes;
    May he be scorned by one, whom all else scorn,
    Forswear to others, what to her he hath sworn,
    With fear of missing, shame of getting, torn:

Madness his sorrow, gout his cramp, may he
Make, by but thinking, who hath made him such:
        And may he feel no touch
        Of conscience, but of fame, and be
Anguished, not that 'twas sin, but that 'twas she:
    In early and long scarceness may he rot,
    For land which had been his, if he had not
    Himself incestuously an heir begot:

May he dream treason, and believe, that he

Meant to perform it, and confess, and die,
     And no record tell why:
     His sons, which none of his may be,
Inherit nothing but his infamy:
  Or may he so long parasites have fed,
  That he would fain be theirs, whom he hath bred,
  And at the last be circumcised for bread:

The venom of all stepdames, gamesters' gall,
What tyrants, and their subjects interwish,
     What plants, mine, beasts, fowl, fish,
     Can contribute, all ill which all
Prophets, or poets spake; and all which shall
  Be annexed in schedules unto this by me,
  Fall on that man; for if it be a she
  Nature beforehand hath out-cursed me.

A Nocturnal upon St. Lucy's Day, Being the Shortest Day

'Tis the year's midnight, and it is the day's,
Lucy's, who scarce seven hours herself unmasks,
  The sun is spent, and now his flasks
  Send forth light squibs, no constant rays;
    The world's whole sap is sunk:
The general balm th'hydroptic earth hath drunk,
Whither, as to the bed's-feet, life is shrunk,
Dead and interred; yet all these seem to laugh,
Compared with me, who am their epitaph.

Study me then, you who shall lovers be
At the next world, that is, at the next spring:
  For I am every dead thing,
  In whom love wrought new alchemy.
    For his art did express
A quintessence even from nothingness,
From dull privations, and lean emptiness:
He ruined me, and I am rebegot
Of absence, darkness, death; things which are not.

All others, from all things, draw all that's good,
Life, soul, form, spirit, whence they being have;
   I, by love's limbeck, am the grave
   Of all, that's nothing. Oft a flood
     Have we two wept, and so
Drowned the whole world, us two; oft did we grow
To be two chaoses, when we did show
Care to aught else; and often absences
Withdrew our souls, and made us carcasses.

But I am by her death (which word wrongs her)
Of the first nothing, the elixir grown;
   Were I a man, that I were one,
   I needs must know; I should prefer,
     If I were any beast,
Some ends, some means; yea plants, yea stones detest,
And love; all, all some properties invest;
If I an ordinary nothing were,
As shadow, a light, and body must be here.

But I am none; nor will my sun renew.
You lovers, for whose sake, the lesser sun
   At this time to the Goat is run
   To fetch new lust, and give it you,
     Enjoy your summer all;
Since she enjoys her long night's festival,
Let me prepare towards her, and let me call
This hour her vigil, and her eve, since this
Both the year's, and the day's deep midnight is.

Witchcraft by a Picture

I fix mine eye on thine, and there
   Pity my picture burning in thine eye,
My picture drowned in a transparent tear,
   When I look lower I espy;
     Hadst thou the wicked skill
By pictures made and marred, to kill,
How many ways mightst thou perform thy will?

But now I have drunk thy sweet salt tears,
    And though thou pour more I'll depart;
My picture vanished, vanish fears,
    That I can be endamaged by that art;
        Though thou retain of me
One picture more, yet that will be,
Being in thine own heart, from all malice free.

The Bait

Come live with me, and be my love,
And we will some new pleasures prove
Of golden sands, and crystal brooks,
With silken lines, and silver hooks.

There will the river whispering run
Warmed by thy eyes, more than the sun.
And there the enamored fish will stay,
Begging themselves they may betray.

When thou wilt swim in that live bath,
Each fish, which every channel hath,
Will amorously to thee swim,
Gladder to catch thee, than thou him.

If thou, to be so seen, be'st loath,
By sun, or moon, thou darkenest both,
And if myself have leave to see,
I need not their light, having thee.

Let others freeze with angling reeds,
And cut their legs, with shells and weeds,
Or treacherously poor fish beset,
With strangling snare, or windowy net:

Let coarse bold hands, from slimy nest
The bedded fish in banks out-wrest,
Or curious traitors, sleavesilk flies
Bewitch poor fishes' wandering eyes.

For thee, thou needst no such deceit,
For thou thyself art thine own bait;
That fish, that is not catched thereby,
Alas, is wiser far than I.

The Apparition

When by thy scorn, O murd'ress, I am dead,
And that thou thinkst thee free
From all solicitation from me,
Then shall my ghost come to thy bed,
And thee, feigned vestal, in worse arms shall see;
Then thy sick taper will begin to wink,
And he, whose thou art then, being tired before,
Will, if thou stir, or pinch to wake him, think
      Thou call'st for more,
And in false sleep will from thee shrink,
And then poor aspen wretch, neglected thou
Bathed in a cold quicksilver sweat wilt lie
      A verier ghost than I;
What I will say, I will not tell thee now,
Lest that preserve thee; and since my love is spent,
I had rather thou shouldst painfully repent,
Than by my threat'nings rest still innocent.

The Broken Heart

He is stark mad, whoever says,
   That he hath been in love an hour,
Yet not that love so soon decays,
   But that it can ten in less space devour;
Who will believe me, if I swear
That I have had the plague a year?
   Who would not laugh at me, if I should say,
   I saw a flask of powder burn a day?

Ah, what a trifle is a heart,
   If once into love's hands it come!
All other griefs allow a part
   To other griefs, and ask themselves but some;
They come to us, but us love draws,
He swallows us, and never chaws:
    By him, as by chained shot, whole ranks do die,
    He is the tyrant pike, our hearts the fry.

If 'twere not so, what did become
   Of my heart, when I first saw thee?
I brought a heart into the room,
   But from the room, I carried none with me:
If it had gone to thee, I know
Mine would have taught thine heart to show
    More pity unto me: but love, alas,
    At one first blow did shiver it as glass.

Yet nothing can to nothing fall,
   Nor any place be empty quite,
Therefore I think my breast hath all
   Those pieces still, though they be not unite;
And now as broken glasses show
A hundred lesser faces, so
    My rags of heart can like, wish, and adore,
    But after one such love, can love no more.

A Valediction: Forbidding Mourning

As virtuous men pass mildly away,
   And whisper to their souls, to go,
Whilst some of their sad friends do say,
   The breath goes now, and some say, no:

So let us melt, and make no noise,
   No tear-floods, nor sigh-tempests move,
'Twere profanation of our joys
   To tell the laity our love.

Moving of th'earth brings harms and fears,
   Men reckon what it did and meant,
But trepidation of the spheres,
   Though greater far, is innocent.

Dull sublunary lovers' love
   (Whose soul is sense) cannot admit
Absence, because it doth remove
   Those things which elemented it.

But we by a love, so much refined,
   That ourselves know not what it is,
Interassured of the mind,
   Care less, eyes, lips, and hands to miss.

Our two souls therefore, which are one,
   Though I must go, endure not yet
A breach, but an expansion,
   Like gold to airy thinness beat.

If they be two, they are two so
   As stiff twin compasses are two,
Thy soul the fixed foot, makes no show
   To move, but doth, if th'other do.

And though it in the center sit,
   Yet when the other far doth roam,
It leans, and hearkens after it,
   And grows erect, as that comes home.

Such wilt thou be to me, who must
   Like th'other foot, obliquely run;
Thy firmness draws my circle just,
   And makes me end, where I begun.

The Ecstasy

Where, like a pillow on a bed,
   A pregnant bank swelled up, to rest
The violet's reclining head,
   Sat we two, one another's best.

Our hands were firmly cemented
   With a fast balm, which thence did spring,
Our eye-beams twisted, and did thread
   Our eyes, upon one double string;
So to'intergraft our hands, as yet
   Was all the means to make us one,
And pictures in our eyes to get
   Was all our propagation.
As 'twixt two equal armies, fate
   Suspends uncertain victory,
Our souls (which to advance their state,
   Were gone out) hung 'twixt her, and me.
And whilst our souls negotiate there,
   We like sepulchral statues lay;
All day, the same our postures were,
   And we said nothing, all the day.
If any, so by love refined,
   That he soul's language understood,
And by good love were grown all mind,
   Within convenient distance stood,
He (though he knew not which soul spake,
   Because both meant, both spake the same)
Might thence a new concoction take,
   And part far purer than he came.
This ecstasy doth unperplex
   (We said) and tell us what we love,
We see by this, it was not sex,
   We see, we saw not what did move:
But as all several souls contain
   Mixture of things, they know not what,
Love, these mixed souls, doth mix again,
   And makes both one, each this and that.
A single violet transplant,
   The strength, the color, and the size,
(All which before was poor, and scant)
   Redoubles still, and multiplies.
When love, with one another so
   Interinanimates two souls,
That abler soul, which thence doth flow,
   Defects of loneliness controls.

We then, who are this new soul, know,
　Of what we are composed, and made,
For, th'atomies of which we grow,
　Are souls, whom no change can invade.
But O alas, so long, so far
　Our bodies why do we forbear?
They are ours, though they are not we, we are
　The intelligences, they the spheres.
We owe them thanks, because they thus,
　Did us, to us, at first convey,
Yielded their forces, sense, to us,
　Nor are dross to us, but allay.
On man heaven's influence works not so,
　But that it first imprints the air,
So soul into the soul may flow,
　Though it to body first repair.
As our blood labors to beget
　Spirits, as like souls as it can,
Because such fingers need to knit
　That subtle knot, which makes us man:
So must pure lovers' souls descend
　T'affections, and to faculties,
Which sense may reach and apprehend,
　Else a great prince in prison lies.
To our bodies turn we then, that so
　Weak men on love revealed may look;
Love's mysteries in souls do grow,
　But yet the body is his book.
And if some lover, such as we,
　Have heard this dialogue of one,
Let him still mark us, he shall see
　Small change, when we are to bodies gone.

Love's Deity

I long to talk with some old lover's ghost,
　Who died before the god of love was born:
I cannot think that he, who then loved most,
　Sunk so low, as to love one which did scorn.

But since this god produced a destiny,
And that vice-nature, custom, lets it be;
   I must love her, that loves not me.

Sure, they which made him god, meant not so much,
   Nor he, in his young godhead practiced it.
But when an even flame two hearts did touch,
   His office was indulgently to fit
Actives to passives. Correspondency
Only his subject was. It cannot be
   Love, till I love her, that loves me.

But every modern god will now extend
   His vast prerogative, as far as Jove.
To rage, to lust, to write to, to commend,
   All is the purlieu of the god of love.
Oh were we wakened by this tyranny
To ungod this child again, it could not be
   I should love her, who loves not me.

Rebel and atheist too, why murmur I,
   As though I felt the worst that love could do?
Love might make me leave loving, or might try
   A deeper plague, to make her love me too,
Which, since she loves before, I am loth to see;
Falsehood is worse than hate; and that must be,
   If she whom I love, should love me.

The Funeral

Whoever comes to shroud me, do not harm
      Nor question much
That subtle wreath of hair, which crowns my arm;
The mystery, the sign you must not touch,
      For 'tis my outward soul,
Viceroy to that, which then to heaven being gone,
      Will leave this to control,
And keep these limbs, her provinces, from dissolution.

For if the sinewy thread my brain lets fall

Through every part,
Can tie those parts, and make me one of all;
These hairs which upward grew, and strength and art
          Have from a better brain,
Can better do it; except she meant that I
          By this should know my pain,
As prisoners then are manacled, when they are condemned to die.

Whate'er she meant by it, bury it with me,
          For since I am
Love's martyr, it might breed idolatry,
If into others' hands these relics came;
          As 'twas humility
To afford to it all that a soul can do,
          So, 'tis some bravery,
That since you would save none of me, I bury some of you.

The Blossom

Little think'st thou, poor flower,
  Whom I have watched six or seven days,
And seen thy birth, and seen what every hour
Gave to thy growth, thee to this height to raise,
And now dost laugh and triumph on this bough,
          Little think'st thou
That it will freeze anon, and that I shall
Tomorrow find thee fall'n, or not at all.

Little think'st thou poor heart
  That labor'st yet to nestle thee,
And think'st by hovering here to get a part
In a forbidden or forbidding tree,
And hop'st her stiffness by long siege to bow:
          Little think'st thou,
That thou tomorrow, ere that sun doth wake,
Must with this sun, and me a journey take.

But thou which lov'st to be
  Subtle to plague thyself, wilt say,

Alas, if you must go, what's that to me?
Here lies my business, and here I will stay:
You go to friends, whose love and means present
      Various content
To your eyes, ears, and tongue, and every part.
If then your body go, what need you a heart?

  Well then, stay here; but know,
   When thou hast stayed and done thy most;
A naked thinking heart, that makes no show,
Is to a woman, but a kind of ghost;
How shall she know my heart; or having none,
      Know thee for one?
Practice may make her know some other part,
But take my word, she doth not know a heart.

  Meet me at London, then,
   Twenty days hence, and thou shalt see
Me fresher, and more fat, by being with men,
Than if I had stayed still with her and thee.
For God's sake, if you can, be you so too:
     I would give you
There, to another friend, whom we shall find
As glad to have my body, as my mind.

The Relic

  When my grave is broke up again
  Some second guest to entertain,
  (For graves have learned that woman-head
  To be to more than one a bed)
    And he that digs it, spies
A bracelet of bright hair about the bone,
    Will he not let us alone,
And think that there a loving couple lies,
Who thought that this device might be some way
To make their souls, at the last busy day,
Meet at this grave, and make a little stay?

If this fall in a time, or land,
Where mis-devotion doth command,
Then, he that digs us up, will bring
Us, to the Bishop, and the King,
   To make us relics; then
Thou shalt be a Mary Magdalen, and I
   A something else thereby;
All women shall adore us, and some men;
And since at such time, miracles are sought,
I would have that age by this paper taught
What miracles we harmless lovers wrought.

  First, we loved well and faithfully,
  Yet knew not what we loved, nor why,
  Difference of sex no more we knew,
  Than our guardian angels do;
   Coming and going, we
Perchance might kiss, but not between those meals;
   Our hands ne'er touched the seals,
Which nature, injured by late law, sets free:
These miracles we did; but now alas,
All measure, and all language, I should pass,
Should I tell what a miracle she was.

A Lecture upon the Shadow

Stand still, and I will read to thee
A lecture, love, in love's philosophy.
  These three hours that we have spent,
  Walking here, two shadows went
Along with us, which we ourselves produced;
But, now the sun is just above our head,
  We do those shadows tread;
  And to brave clearness all things are reduced.
 So whilst our infant loves did grow,
 Disguises did, and shadows, flow,
From us, and our cares; but, now 'tis not so.

That love hath not attained the high'st degree,
Which is still diligent lest others see.

Except our loves at this noon stay,
We shall new shadows make the other way.
    As the first were made to blind
    Others; these which come behind
Will work upon ourselves, and blind our eyes.
If our loves faint, and westwardly decline;
    To me thou, falsely, thine,
    And I to thee mine actions shall disguise.
The morning shadows wear away,
But these grow longer all the day,
But oh, love's day is short, if love decay.

Love is a growing, or full constant light;
And his first minute, after noon, is night.

A Burnt Ship

Out of a fired ship, which, by no way
But drowning, could be rescued from the flame,
Some men leaped forth, and ever as they came
Near the foes' ships, did by their shot decay;
So all were lost, which in the ship were found,
    They in the sea being burnt, they in the burnt ship drowned.

Fall of a Wall

Under an undermined, and shot-bruised wall
A too-bold captain perished by the fall,
Whose brave misfortune, happiest men envied,
That had a town for tomb, his bones to hide.

Cales* and Guiana

If you from spoil of th'old world's farthest end
To the new world your kindled valors bend,
What brave examples then do prove it true
That one thing's end doth still begin a new.

An Obscure Writer

Philo, with twelve years' study, hath been grieved
To be understood; when will he be believed?

The Liar

Thou in the fields walkst out thy supping hours
  And yet thou swear'st thou hast supped like a king:
Like Nebuchadnezzar perchance with grass and flowers,
  A salad worse than Spanish dieting.

Elegy I: Jealousy

Fond woman, which wouldst have thy husband die,
And yet complain'st of his great jealousy;
If swoll'n with poison, he lay in his last bed,
His body with a sere-bark covered,
Drawing his breath, as thick and short, as can
The nimblest crocheting musician,
Ready with loathsome vomiting to spew
His soul out of one hell, into a new,
Made deaf with his poor kindred's howling cries,
Begging with few feigned tears, great legacies,

---

* Cadiz.

Thou wouldst not weep, but jolly, and frolic be,
As a slave, which tomorrow should be free;
Yet weep'st thou, when thou seest him hungerly
Swallow his own death, heart's-bane jealousy.
O give him many thanks, he is courteous,
That in suspecting kindly warneth us.
We must not, as we used, flout openly,
In scoffing riddles, his deformity;
Nor at his board together being sat,
With words, nor touch, scarce looks adulterate.
Nor when he swoll'n, and pampered with great fare
Sits down, and snorts, caged in his basket chair,
Must we usurp his own bed any more,
Nor kiss and play in his house, as before.
Now I see many dangers; for that is
His realm, his castle, and his diocese.
But if, as envious men, which would revile
Their prince, or coin his gold, themselves exile
Into another country, and do it there,
We play in another house, what should we fear?
There we will scorn his household policies,
His silly plots, and pensionary spies,
As the inhabitants of Thames' right side
Do London's Mayor; or Germans, the Pope's pride.

Elegy II: The Anagram

Marry, and love thy Flavia, for, she
Hath all things, whereby others beauteous be,
For, though her eyes be small, her mouth is great,
Though they be ivory, yet her teeth be jet,
Though they be dim, yet she is light enough,
And though her harsh hair fall, her skin is rough;
What though her cheeks be yellow, her hair's red,
Give her thine, and she hath a maidenhead.
These things are beauty's elements, where these
Meet in one, that one must, as perfect, please.
If red and white and each good quality

Be in thy wench, ne'er ask where it doth lie.
In buying things perfumed, we ask, if there
Be musk and amber in it, but not where.
Though all her parts be not in th'usual place,
She hath yet an anagram of a good face.
If we might put the letters but one way,
In the lean dearth of words, what could we say?
When by the gamut some musicians make
A perfect song, others will undertake,
By the same gamut changed, to equal it.
Things simply good, can never be unfit.
She's fair as any, if all be like her,
And if none be, then she is singular.
All love is wonder; if we justly do
Account her wonderful, why not lovely too?
Love built on beauty, soon as beauty, dies,
Choose this face, changed by no deformities.
Women are all like angels; the fair be
Like those which fell to worse; but such as thee,
Like to good angels, nothing can impair:
'Tis less grief to be foul, than to have been fair.
For one night's revels, silk and gold we choose,
But, in long journeys, cloth, and leather use.
Beauty is barren oft; best husbands say,
There is best land, where there is foulest way.
Oh what a sovereign plaster will she be,
If thy past sins have taught thee jealousy!
Here needs no spies, nor eunuchs; her commit
Safe to thy foes; yea, to a marmoset.
When Belgia's cities, the round countries drown,
That dirty foulness guards, and arms the town:
So doth her face guard her; and so, for thee,
Which, forced by business, absent oft must be,
She, whose face, like clouds, turns the day to night,
Who, mightier than the sea, makes Moors seem white,
Who, though seven years, she in the stews had laid,
A nunnery durst receive, and think a maid,
And though in childbed's labor she did lie,
Midwives would swear, 'twere but a tympany,
Whom, if she accuse herself, I credit less

Than witches, which impossibles confess,
Whom dildoes, bedstaves, and her velvet glass
Would be as loth to touch as Joseph was:
One like none, and liked of none, fittest were,
For, things in fashion every man will wear.

Elegy V: His Picture

Here take my picture; though I bid farewell,
Thine, in my heart, where my soul dwells, shall dwell.
'Tis like me now, but I dead, 'twill be more
When we are shadows both, than 'twas before.
When weather-beaten I come back; my hand,
Perhaps with rude oars torn, or sunbeams tanned,
My face and breast of haircloth, and my head
With care's rash sudden storms, being o'erspread,
My body a sack of bones, broken within,
And powder's blue stains scattered on my skin;
If rival fools tax thee to have loved a man,
So foul, and coarse, as, oh, I may seem then,
This shall say what I was: and thou shalt say,
Do his hurts reach me? doth my worth decay?
Or do they reach his judging mind, that he
Should now love less, what he did love to see?
That which in him was fair and delicate,
Was but the milk, which in love's childish state
Did nurse it: who now is grown strong enough
To feed on that, which to disused tastes seems tough.

Elegy IX: The Autumnal

No spring, nor summer beauty hath such grace,
    As I have seen in one autumnal face.
Young beauties force our love, and that's a rape,
    This doth but counsel, yet you cannot 'scape.
If 'twere a shame to love, here 'twere no shame,

Affection here takes reverence's name.
Were her first years the Golden Age; that's true,
   But now she's gold oft tried, and ever new.
That was her torrid and enflaming time,
   This is her tolerable tropic clime.
Fair eyes, who asks more heat than comes from hence,
   He in a fever wishes pestilence.
Call not these wrinkles, graves; if graves they were,
   They were love's graves; for else he is nowhere.
Yet lies not love dead here, but here doth sit
   Vowed to this trench, like an anachorit.*
And here, till hers, which must be his death, come,
   He doth not dig a grave, but build a tomb.
Here dwells he, though he sojourn everywhere,
   In progress, yet his standing house is here.
Here, where still evening is; not noon, nor night;
   Where no voluptuousness, yet all delight.
In all her words, unto all hearers fit,
   You may at revels, you at council, sit.
This is love's timber, youth his underwood;
   There he, as wine in June, enrages blood,
Which then comes seasonabliest, when our taste
   And appetite to other things, is past.
Xerxes' strange Lydian love, the platan tree,
   Was loved for age, none being so large as she,
Or else because, being young, nature did bless
   Her youth with age's glory, barrenness.
If we love things long sought, age is a thing
   Which we are fifty years in compassing.
If transitory things, which soon decay,
   Age must be loveliest at the latest day.
But name not winter-faces, whose skin's slack;
   Lank, as an unthrift's purse; but a soul's sack;
Whose eyes seek light within, for all here's shade;
   Whose mouths are holes, rather worn out, than made;
Whose every tooth to a several place is gone,
   To vex their souls at Resurrection;

---

* Anchorite.

Name not these living death's-heads unto me,
  For these, not ancient, but antique be.
I hate extremes; yet I had rather stay
  With tombs, than cradles, to wear out a day.
Since such love's natural lation* is, may still
  My love descend, and journey down the hill,
Not panting after growing beauties, so,
  I shall ebb out with them, who homeward go.

Elegy XVI: On His Mistress

By our first strange and fatal interview,
By all desires which thereof did ensue,
By our long starving hopes, by that remorse
Which my words' masculine persuasive force
Begot in thee, and by the memory
Of hurts, which spies and rivals threatened me,
I calmly beg: but by thy father's wrath,
By all pains, which want and divorcement hath,
I conjure thee, and all the oaths which I
And thou have sworn to seal joint constancy,
Here I unswear, and overswear them thus,
Thou shalt not love by ways so dangerous.
Temper, O fair love, love's impetuous rage,
Be my true mistress still, not my feigned page;
I'll go, and, by thy kind leave, leave behind
Thee, only worthy to nurse in my mind,
Thirst to come back; O if thou die before,
My soul from other lands to thee shall soar.
Thy (else almighty) beauty cannot move
Rage from the seas, nor thy love teach them love,
Nor tame wild Boreas' harshness; thou hast read
How roughly he in pieces shivered
Fair Orithea, whom he swore he loved.
Fall ill or good, 'tis madness to have proved

---

* Movement.

Dangers unurged; feed on this flattery,
That absent lovers one in th'other be.
Dissemble nothing, not a boy, nor change
Thy body's habit, nor mind's; be not strange
To thyself only; all will spy in thy face
A blushing womanly discovering grace;
Richly clothed apes are called apes, and as soon
Eclipsed as bright we call the moon the moon.
Men of France, changeable chameleons,
Spitals of diseases, shops of fashions,
Love's fuelers, and the rightest company
Of players, which upon the world's stage be,
Will quickly know thee, and no less, alas!
Th'indifferent Italian, as we pass
His warm land, well content to think thee page,
Will hunt thee with such lust, and hideous rage,
As Lot's fair guests were vexed. But none of these
Nor spongy hydroptic Dutch shall thee displease,
If thou stay here. O stay here, for, for thee
England is only a worthy gallery,
To walk in expectation, till from thence
Our greatest King call thee to his presence.
When I am gone, dream me some happiness,
Nor let thy looks our long hid love confess,
Nor praise, nor dispraise me, nor bless nor curse
Openly love's force, nor in bed fright thy nurse
With midnight's startings, crying out, "Oh, oh
Nurse, O my love is slain, I saw him go
O'er the white Alps alone; I saw him, I,
Assailed, fight, taken, stabbed, bleed, fall, and die."
Augur me better chance, except dread Jove
Think it enough for me to have had thy love.

Elegy XIX: To His Mistress Going to Bed

Come, Madam, come, all rest my powers defy,
Until I labor, I in labor lie.
The foe oft-times, having the foe in sight,
Is tired with standing though he never fight.

Off with that girdle, like heaven's zone glistering,
But a far fairer world encompassing.
Unpin that spangled breastplate which you wear,
That th'eyes of busy fools may be stopped there.
Unlace yourself, for that harmonious chime
Tells me from you, that now it is bedtime.
Off with that happy busk, which I envy,
That still can be, and still can stand so nigh.
Your gown going off, such beauteous state reveals,
As when from flowery meads th'hill's shadow steals.
Off with that wiry coronet and show
The hairy diadem which on you doth grow:
Now off with those shoes, and then safely tread
In this love's hallowed temple, this soft bed.
In such white robes, heaven's angels used to be
Received by men; thou angel bringst with thee
A heaven like Mahomet's paradise; and though
Ill spirits walk in white, we easily know,
By this these angels from an evil sprite,
Those set our hairs, but these our flesh upright.
    Licence my roving hands, and let them go,
Before, behind, between, above, below.
O my America! my new found land,
My kingdom, safeliest when with one man manned,
My mine of precious stones, my empery,
How blessed am I in this discovering thee!
To enter in these bonds, is to be free;
Then where my hand is set, my seal shall be.
    Full nakedness! All joys are due to thee;
As souls unbodied, bodies unclothed must be,
To taste whole joys. Gems which you women use
Are like Atlanta's balls, cast in men's views,
That when a fool's eye lighteth on a gem,
His earthly soul may covet theirs, not them.
Like pictures, or like books' gay coverings made
For laymen, are all women thus arrayed;
Themselves are mystic books, which only we
(Whom their imputed grace will dignify)
Must see revealed. Then since that I may know;
As liberally, as to a midwife, show

Thyself: cast all, yea, this white linen hence,
There is no penance due to innocence.
　　To teach thee, I am naked first; why then
What needst thou have more covering than a man?

An Epithalamion, or Marriage Song on the Lady Elizabeth and Count Palatine Being Married on St. Valentine's Day

Hail Bishop Valentine, whose day this is,
　　　　All the air is thy diocese,
　　　　And all the chirping choristers
And other birds are thy parishioners,
　　　　Thou marriest every year
The lyric lark, and the grave whispering dove,
The sparrow that neglects his life for love,
The household bird, with the red stomacher,
　　　　Thou mak'st the blackbird speed as soon,
As doth the goldfinch, or the halcyon;
The husband cock looks out, and straight is sped,
And meets his wife, which brings her feather-bed.
This day more cheerfully than ever shine,
This day, which might enflame thyself, old Valentine.

Till now, thou warmed'st with multiplying loves
　　　　Two larks, two sparrows, or two doves;
　　　　All that is nothing unto this,
For thou this day couplest two phoenixes;
　　　　Thou mak'st a taper see
What the sun never saw, and what the ark
(Which was of fowls, and beasts, the cage, and park)
Did not contain, one bed contains, through thee,
　　　　Two phoenixes, whose joined breasts
Are unto one another mutual nests,
Where motion kindles such fires, as shall give
Young phoenixes, and yet the old shall live.
Whose love and courage never shall decline,
But make the whole year through, thy day, O Valentine.

Up then fair phoenix bride, frustrate the sun,
      Thyself from thine affection
      Takest warmth enough, and from thine eye
All lesser birds will take their jollity.
        Up, up, fair bride, and call,
Thy stars, from out their several boxes, take
Thy rubies, pearls, and diamonds forth, and make
Thyself a constellation, of them all,
      And by their blazing, signify,
That a great princess falls, but doth not die;
Be thou a new star, that to us portends
Ends of much wonder; and be thou those ends.
Since thou dost this day in new glory shine,
May all men date records, from this thy Valentine.

Come forth, come forth, and as one glorious flame
      Meeting another, grows the same,
      So meet thy Frederick, and so
To an unseparable union grow.
      Since separation
Falls not on such things as are infinite,
Nor things which are but one, can disunite,
You are twice inseparable, great, and one;
      Go then to where the bishop stays,
To make you one, his way, which divers ways
Must be effected; and when all is past,
And that you are one, by hearts and hands made fast,
You two have one way left, yourselves to entwine,
Besides this bishop's knot, or Bishop Valentine.

But oh, what ails the sun, that here he stays,
      Longer today, than other days?
      Stays he new light from these to get?
And finding here such store, is loth to set?
      And why do you two walk,
So slowly paced in this procession?
Is all your care but to be looked upon,
And be to others spectacle, and talk?
      The feast, with gluttonous delays,
Is eaten, and too long their meat they praise,
The masquers come too late, and I think, will stay,

Like fairies, till the cock crow them away.
Alas, did not antiquity assign
A night, as well as day, to thee, O Valentine?

They did, and night is come; and yet we see
        Formalities retarding thee.
        What mean these ladies, which (as though
They were to take a clock in pieces) go
        So nicely about the bride;
A bride, before a good night could be said,
Should vanish from her clothes, into her bed,
As souls from bodies steal, and are spied.
        But now she is laid; what though she be?
Yet there are more delays, for, where is he?
He comes, and passes through sphere after sphere,
First her sheets, then her arms, then anywhere.
Let not this day, then, but this night be thine,
Thy day was but the eve to this, O Valentine.

Here lies a she sun, and a he moon here,
        She gives the best light to his sphere,
        Or each is both, and all, and so
They unto one another nothing owe,
        And yet they do, but are
So just and rich in that coin which they pay,
That neither would, nor needs forbear nor stay;
Neither desires to be spared, nor to spare,
        They quickly pay their debt, and then
Take no acquittances, but pay again;
They pay, they give, they lend, and so let fall
No such occasion to be liberal.
More truth, more courage in these two do shine,
Than all thy turtles have, and sparrows, Valentine.

And by this act of these two phoenixes
        Nature again restored is,
        For since these two are two no more,
There's but one phoenix still, as was before.
        Rest now at last, and we
As satyrs watch the sun's uprise, will stay
Waiting, when your eyes opened, let out day,

Only desired, because your face we see;
       Others near you shall whispering speak,
And wagers lay, at which side day will break,
And win by observing, then, whose hand it is
That opens first a curtain, hers or his;
This will be tried tomorrow after nine,
Till which hour, we thy day enlarge, O Valentine.

Satire I

Away thou fondling motley humorist,
Leave me, and in this standing wooden chest,
Consorted with these few books, let me lie
In prison, and here be coffined, when I die;
Here are God's conduits, grave divines; and here
Nature's secretary, the philosopher;
And jolly statesmen, which teach how to tie
The sinews of a city's mystic body;
Here gathering chroniclers, and by them stand
Giddy fantastic poets of each land.
Shall I leave all this constant company,
And follow headlong, wild uncertain thee?
First swear by thy best love in earnest
(If thou which lov'st all, canst love any best)
Thou wilt not leave me in the middle street,
Though some more spruce companion thou dost meet,
Not though a captain do come in thy way
Bright parcel gilt, with forty dead men's pay,
Not though a brisk perfumed pert courtier
Deign with a nod, thy courtesy to answer.
Nor come a velvet justice with a long
Great train of blue coats, twelve, or fourteen strong,
Wilt thou grin or fawn on him, or prepare
A speech to court his beauteous son and heir!
For better or worse take me, or leave me:
To take, and leave me is adultery.
Oh monstrous, superstitious Puritan,
Of refined manners, yet ceremonial man,

That when thou meet'st one, with inquiring eyes
Dost search, and like a needy broker prize
The silk, and gold he wears, and to that rate
So high or low, dost raise thy formal hat:
That wilt comfort none, until thou have known
What lands he hath in hope, or of his own,
As though all thy companions should make thee
Jointures, and marry thy dear company.
Why shouldst thou (that dost not only approve,
But in rank itchy lust, desire, and love
The nakedness and bareness to enjoy,
Of thy plump muddy whore, or prostitute boy)
Hate virtue, though she be naked, and bare?
At birth, and death, our bodies naked arc;
And till our souls be unapparelled
Of bodies, they from bliss are banished.
Man's first blessed state was naked, when by sin
He lost that, yet he was clothed but in beast's skin,
And in this coarse attire, which I now wear,
With God, and with the Muses I confer.
But since thou like a contrite penitent,
Charitably warned of thy sins, dost repent
These vanities, and giddinesses, lo
I shut my chamber door, and come, let's go.
But sooner may a cheap whore, who hath been
Worn by as many several men in sin,
As are black feathers, or musk-color hose,
Name her child's right true father, 'mongst all those:
Sooner may one guess, who shall bear away
The Infanta of London, heir to an India;
And sooner may a gulling weather spy
By drawing forth heaven's scheme tell certainly
What fashioned hats, or ruffs, or suits next year
Our subtle-witted antic youths will wear;
Than thou, when thou depart'st from me, canst show
Whither, why, when, or with whom thou wouldst go.
But how shall I be pardoned my offence
That thus have sinned against my conscience?
Now we are in the street; he first of all
Improvidently proud, creeps to the wall,

And so imprisoned, and hemmed in by me
Sells for a little state his liberty;
Yet though he cannot skip forth now to greet
Every fine silken painted fool we meet,
He them to him with amorous smiles allures,
And grins, smacks, shrugs, and such an itch endures,
As prentices, or schoolboys which do know
Of some gay sport abroad, yet dare not go.
And as fiddlers stop lowest, at highest sound,
So to the most brave, stoops he nigh'st the ground.
But to a grave man, he doth move no more
Than the wise politic horse would heretofore,
Or thou O elephant or ape wilt do,
When any names the King of Spain to you.
Now leaps he upright, jogs me, and cries, "Do you see
Yonder well-favored youth? Oh, 'tis he
That dances so divinely." "Oh," said I,
"Stand still, must you dance here for company?"
He drooped, we went, till one (which did excel
Th'Indians, in drinking his tobacco well)
Met us; they talked; I whispered, "Let us go,
'T may be you smell him not, truly I do."
He hears not me, but, on the other side
A many-colored peacock having spied,
Leaves him and me; I for my lost sheep stay;
He follows, overtakes, goes on the way,
Saying, "Him whom I last left, all repute
For his device, in handsoming a suit,
To judge of lace, pink, panes, print, cut, and pleat
Of all the Court to have the best conceit."
"Our dull comedians want him, let him go;
But oh, God strengthen thee, why stoop'st thou so?"
"Why? he hath traveled." "Long?" "No; but to me"
(Which understand none) "he doth seem to be
Perfect French, and Italian." I replied,
"So is the pox." He answered not, but spied
More men of sort, of parts, and qualities;
At last his love he in a window spies,
And like light dew exhaled, he flings from me
Violently ravished to his lechery.

Many were there, he could command no more;
He quarreled, fought, bled; and turned out of door
    Directly came to me hanging the head,
    And constantly a while must keep his bed.

Satire III

Kind pity chokes my spleen; brave scorn forbids
Those tears to issue which swell my eyelids;
I must not laugh, nor weep sins, and be wise,
Can railing then cure these worn maladies?
Is not our mistress fair religion,
As worthy of all our soul's devotion,
As virtue was to the first blinded age?
Are not heaven's joys as valiant to assuage
Lusts, as earth's honor was to them? Alas,
As we do them in means, shall they surpass
Us in the end, and shall thy father's spirit
Meet blind philosophers in heaven, whose merit
Of strict life may be imputed faith, and hear
Thee, whom he taught so easy ways and near
To follow, damned? O if thou dar'st, fear this;
This fear great courage, and high valor is.
Dar'st thou aid mutinous Dutch, and dar'st thou lay
Thee in ships' wooden sepulchers, a prey
To leaders' rage, to storms, to shot, to dearth?
Dar'st thou dive seas, and dungeons of the earth?
Hast thou courageous fire to thaw the ice
Of frozen north discoveries? and thrice
Colder than salamanders, like divine
Children in th'oven, fires of Spain, and the line,
Whose countries limbecks to our bodies be,
Canst thou for gain bear? and must every he
Which cries not, "Goddess," to thy mistress, draw,
Or eat thy poisonous words? courage of straw!
O desperate coward, wilt thou seem bold, and
To thy foes and his (who made thee to stand

Sentinel in his world's garrison) thus yield,
And for the forbidden wars, leave th'appointed field?
Know thy foes: the foul devil (whom thou
Strivest to please), for hate, not love, would allow
Thee fain, his whole realm to be quit; and as
The world's all parts wither away and pass,
So the world's self, thy other loved foe, is
In her decrepit wane, and thou loving this,
Dost love a withered and worn strumpet; last,
Flesh (itself's death) and joys which flesh can taste,
Thou lovest; and thy fair goodly soul, which doth
Give this flesh power to taste joy, thou dost loathe.
Seek true religion. O where? Mirreus
Thinking her unhoused here, and fled from us,
Seeks her at Rome; there, because he doth know
That she was there a thousand years ago,
He loves her rags so, as we here obey
The statecloth where the prince sat yesterday.
Crants to such brave loves will not be enthralled,
But loves her only, who at Geneva is called
Religion, plain, simple, sullen, young,
Contemptuous, yet unhandsome; as among
Lecherous humors, there is one that judges
No wenches wholesome, but coarse country drudges.
Graius stays still at home here, and because
Some preachers, vile ambitious bawds, and laws
Still new like fashions, bid him think that she
Which dwells with us, is only perfect, he
Embraceth her, whom his godfathers will
Tender to him, being tender, as wards still
Take such wives as their guardians offer, or
Pay values. Careless Phrygius doth abhor
All, because all cannot be good, as one
Knowing some women whores, dares marry none.
Gracchus loves all as one, and thinks that so
As women do in divers countries go
In divers habits, yet are still one kind,
So doth, so is religion; and this blind-
ness too much light breeds; but unmoved thou
Of force must one, and forced but one allow;

And the right; ask thy father which is she,
Let him ask his; though truth and falsehood be
Near twins, yet truth a little elder is;
Be busy to seek her, believe me this,
He's not of none, nor worst, that seeks the best.
To adore, or scorn an image, or protest,
May all be bad; doubt wisely; in strange way
To stand inquiring right, is not to stray;
To sleep, or run wrong, is. On a huge hill,
Cragged, and steep, truth stands, and he that will
Reach her, about must, and about must go;
And what the hill's suddenness resists, win so;
Yet strive so, that before age, death's twilight,
Thy soul rest, for none can work in that night.
To will, implies delay, therefore now do:
Hard deeds, the body's pains; hard knowledge too
The mind's endeavors reach, and mysteries
Are like the sun, dazzling, yet plain to all eyes.
Keep the truth which thou hast found; men do not stand
In so ill case here, that God hath with his hand
Signed kings blank-charters to kill whom they hate,
Nor are they vicars, but hangmen to fate.
Fool and wretch, wilt thou let thy soul be tied
To man's laws, by which she shall not be tried
At the last day? Oh, will it then boot thee
To say a Philip, or a Gregory,
A Harry, or a Martin taught thee this?
Is not this excuse for mere contraries,
Equally strong? cannot both sides say so?
That thou mayest rightly obey power, her bounds know;
Those past, her nature, and name is changed; to be
Then humble to her is idolatry.
As streams are, power is; those blessed flowers that dwell
At the rough stream's calm head, thrive and do well,
But having left their roots, and themselves given
To the stream's tyrannous rage, alas, are driven
Through mills, and rocks, and woods, and at last, almost
Consumed in going, in the sea are lost:
So perish souls, which more choose men's unjust
Power from God claimed, than God himself to trust.

To Mr. Christopher Brooke

THE STORM

Thou which art I, ('tis nothing to be so)
Thou which art still thyself, by these shalt know
Part of our passage; and, a hand, or eye
By Hilliard drawn, is worth an history,
By a worse painter made; and (without pride)
When by thy judgment they are dignified,
My lines are such: 'tis the preeminence
Of friendship only to impute excellence.
England to whom we owe, what we be, and have,
Sad that her sons did seek a foreign grave
(For, fate's, or fortune's drifts none can soothsay,
Honor and misery have one face and way)
From out her pregnant entrails sighed a wind
Which at th'air's middle marble room did find
Such strong resistance, that itself it threw
Downward again; and so when it did view
How in the port, our fleet dear time did leese,
Withering like prisoners, which lie but for fees,
Mildly it kissed our sails, and, fresh and sweet,
As to a stomach starved, whose insides meet,
Meat comes, it came; and swole our sails, when we
So joyed, as Sara her swelling joyed to see.
But 'twas but so kind, as our countrymen,
Which bring friends one day's way, and leave them then.
Then like two mighty kings, which dwelling far
Asunder, meet against a third to war,
The south and west winds joined, and, as they blew,
Waves like a rolling trench before them threw.
Sooner than you read this line, did the gale,
Like shot, not feared till felt, our sails assail;
And what at first was called a gust, the same
Hath now a storm's, anon a tempest's name.
Jonas, I pity thee, and curse those men,
Who when the storm raged most, did wake thee then;
Sleep is pain's easiest salve, and doth fulfill
All offices of death, except to kill.

But when I waked, I saw, that I saw not;
Ay, and the sun, which should teach me had forgot
East, west, day, night, and I could only say,
If the world had lasted, now it had been day.
Thousands our noises were, yet we 'mongst all
Could none by his right name, but thunder call:
Lightning was all our light, and it rained more
Than if the sun had drunk the sea before.
Some coffined in their cabins lie, equally
Grieved that they are not dead, and yet must die;
And as sin-burdened souls from graves will creep,
At the last day, some forth their cabins peep:
And tremblingly ask what news, and do hear so,
Like jealous husbands, what they would not know.
Some sitting on the hatches, would seem there,
With hideous gazing to fear away fear.
Then note they the ship's sicknesses, the mast
Shaked with this ague, and the hold and waist
With a salt dropsy clogged, and all our tacklings
Snapping, like too high stretched treble strings.
And from our tottered sails, rags drop down so,
As from one hanged in chains, a year ago.
Even our ordnance placed for our defense,
Strive to break loose, and 'scape away from thence.
Pumping hath tired our men, and what's the gain?
Seas into seas thrown, we suck in again;
Hearing hath deafed our sailors; and if they
Knew how to hear, there's none knows what to say.
Compared to these storms, death is but a qualm,
Hell somewhat lightsome, and the Bermuda calm.
Darkness, light's elder brother, his birthright
Claims o'er this world, and to heaven hath chased light.
All things are one, and that one none can be,
Since all forms, uniform deformity
Doth cover, so that we, except God say
Another *Fiat*,* shall have no more day.
So violent, yet long these furies be,
That though thine absence starve me, I wish not thee.

---

* Let there be.

THE CALM

Our storm is past, and that storm's tyrannous rage,
A stupid calm, but nothing it, doth 'suage.
The fable is inverted, and far more
A block afflicts, now, than a stork before.
Storms chafe, and soon wear out themselves, or us;
In calms, heaven laughs to see us languish thus.
As steady as I can wish, that my thoughts were,
Smooth as thy mistress' glass, or what shines there,
The sea is now. And, as the Isles which we
Seek, when we can move, our ships rooted be.
As water did in storms, now pitch runs out:
As lead, when a fired church becomes one spout.
And all our beauty, and our trim, decays,
Like courts removing, or like ended plays.
The fighting place now seamen's rags supply;
And all the tackling is a frippery.
No use of lanthorns; and in one place lay
Feathers and dust, today and yesterday.
Earth's hollownesses, which the world's lungs are,
Have no more wind than the upper vault of air.
We can nor lost friends, nor sought foes recover,
But meteorlike, save that we move not, hover.
Only the calenture* together draws
Dear friends, which meet dead in great fishes' jaws:
And on the hatches as on altars lies
Each one, his own priest, and own sacrifice.
Who live, that miracle do multiply
Where walkers in hot ovens, do not die.
If in despite of these, we swim, that hath
No more refreshing, than our brimstone bath,
But from the sea, into the ship we turn,
Like parboiled wretches, on the coals to burn.
Like Bajazet encaged, the shepherd's scoff,
Or like slack-sinewed Sampson, his hair off,

---

* A madness impelling sailors to jump overboard.

Languish our ships. Now, as a myriad
Of ants, durst th'emperor's loved snake invade,
The crawling galleys, sea-gaols, finny chips,
Might brave our pinnaces, now bed-rid ships.
Whether a rotten state, and hope of gain,
Or to disuse me from the queasy pain
Of being beloved, and loving, or the thirst
Of honor, or fair death, out pushed me first,
I lose my end: for here as well as I
A desperate may live, and a coward die.
Stag, dog, and all which from, or towards flies,
Is paid with life, or prey, or doing dies.
Fate grudges us all, and doth subtly lay
A scourge, 'gainst which we all forget to pray,
He that at sea prays for more wind, as well
Under the poles may beg cold, heat in hell.
What are we then? How little more alas
Is man now, than before he was? he was
Nothing; for us, we are for nothing fit;
Chance, or ourselves still disproportion it.
We have no power, no will, no sense; I lie,
I should not then thus feel this misery.

To Mr. Rowland Woodward

Like one who in her third widowhood doth profess
Herself a nun, tied to retiredness,
So affects my Muse now, a chaste fallowness;

Since she to few, yet to too many hath shown
How love-song weeds, and satiric thorns are grown
Where seeds of better arts, were early sown.

Though to use, and love poetry, to me,
Betrothed to no one art, be no adultery;
Omissions of good, ill, as ill deeds be.

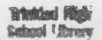

For though to us it seem, and be light and thin,
Yet in those faithful scales, where God throws in
Men's works, vanity weighs as much as sin.

If our souls have stained their first white, yet we
May clothe them with faith, and dear honesty,
Which God imputes, as native purity.

There is no virtue, but religion:
Wise, valiant, sober, just, are names, which none
Want, which want not vice-covering discretion.

Seek we then ourselves in ourselves; for as
Men force the sun with much more force to pass,
By gathering his beams with a crystal glass;

So we, if we into ourselves will turn,
Blowing our sparks of virtue, may outburn
The straw, which doth about our hearts sojourn.

You know, physicians, when they would infuse
Into any oil, the souls of simples, use
Places, where they may lie still warm, to choose.

So works retiredness in us; to roam
Giddily, and be everywhere, but at home,
Such freedom doth a banishment become.

We are but farmers of ourselves, yet may,
If we can stock ourselves, and thrive, uplay
Much, much dear treasure for the great rent day.

Manure thyself then, to thyself be approved,
And with vain outward things be no more moved,
But to know, that I love thee and would be loved.

To the Countess of Bedford on New Year's Day

This twilight of two years, not past nor next,
    Some emblem is of me, or I of this,
Who meteorlike, of stuff and form perplexed,
    Whose what, and where, in disputation is,

If I should call me anything, should miss.

I sum the years, and me, and find me not
   Debtor to th'old, nor creditor to the new,
That cannot say, my thanks I have forgot,
   Nor trust I this with hopes, and yet scarce true
   This bravery is, since these times showed me you.

In recompense I would show future times
   What you were, and teach them to urge towards such.
Verse embalms virtue; and tombs, or thrones of rhymes,
   Preserve frail transitory fame, as much
   As spice doth bodies from corrupt air's touch.

Mine are short-lived; the tincture of your name
   Creates in them, but dissipates as fast,
New spirits: for, strong agents with the same
   Force that doth warm and cherish, us do waste;
   Kept hot with strong extracts, no bodies last:

So, my verse built of your just praise, might want
   Reason and likelihood, the firmest base,
And made of miracle, now faith is scant,
   Will vanish soon, and so possess no place,
   And you, and it, too much grace might disgrace.

When all (as truth commands assent) confess
   All truth of you, yet they will doubt how I,
One corn of one low anthill's dust, and less,
   Should name, know, or express a thing so high,
   And not an inch, measure infinity.

I cannot tell them, nor myself, nor you,
   But leave, lest truth be endangered by my praise,
And turn to God, who knows I think this true,
   And useth oft, when such a heart mis-says,
   To make it good, for, such a praiser prays.

He will best teach you, how you should lay out
   His stock of beauty, learning, favor, blood;
He will perplex security with doubt,
   And clear those doubts; hide from you, and show you good,
   And so increase your appetite and food;

He will teach you, that good and bad have not
   One latitude in cloisters, and in Court;
Indifferent there the greatest space hath got;
    Some pity is not good there, some vain disport,
    On this side sin, with that place may comport.

Yet he, as he bounds seas, will fix your hours,
   Which pleasure, and delight may not ingress,
And though what none else lost, be truliest yours,
    He will make you, what you did not, possess,
    By using others', not vice, but weakness.

He will make you speak truths, and credibly,
   And make you doubt, that others do not so:
He will provide you keys, and locks, to spy,
    And 'scape spies, to good ends, and he will show
    What you may not acknowledge, what not know.

For your own conscience, he gives innocence,
   But for your fame, a discreet wariness,
And though to 'scape, than to revenge offence
    Be better, he shows both, and to repress
    Joy, when your state swells, sadness when 'tis less.

From need of tears he will defend your soul,
   Or make a rebaptizing of one tear;
He cannot, (that's, he will not) disenrol
    Your name; and when with active joy we hear
    This private gospel, then 'tis our New Year.

Elegy on the Lady Markham

Man is the world, and death the ocean,
   To which God gives the lower parts of man.
This sea environs all, and though as yet
   God hath set marks, and bounds, 'twixt us and it,
Yet doth it roar, and gnaw, and still pretend,
   And breaks our banks, whene'er it takes a friend.
Then our land waters (tears of passion) vent;
   Our waters, then, above our firmament,

(Tears which our soul doth for her sins let fall)
   Take all a brackish taste, and funeral,
And even these tears, which should wash sin, are sin.
   We, after God's "No," drown our world again.
Nothing but man of all envenomed things
   Doth work upon itself, with inborn stings.
Tears are false spectacles, we cannot see
   Through passion's mist, what we are, or what she.
In her this sea of death hath made no breach,
   But as the tide doth wash the slimy beach,
And leaves embroidered works upon the sand,
   So is her flesh refined by death's cold hand.
As men of China, after an age's stay,
   Do take up porcelain, where they buried clay;
So at this grave, her limbeck, which refines
   The diamonds, rubies, sapphires, pearls, and mines,
Of which this flesh was, her soul shall inspire
   Flesh of such stuff, as God, when his last fire
Annuls this world, to recompense it, shall,
   Make and name then, th' elixir of this all.
They say, the sea, when it gains, loseth too;
   If carnal death (the younger brother) do
Usurp the body, our soul, which subject is
   To th'elder death, by sin, is freed by this;
They perish both, when they attempt the just;
   For, graves our trophies are, and both deaths' dust.
So, unobnoxious now, she hath buried both;
   For, none to death sins, that to sin is loth,
Nor do they die, which are not loth to die;
   So hath she this, and that virginity.
Grace was in her extremely diligent,
   That kept her from sin, yet made her repent.
Of what small spots pure white complains! Alas,
   How little poison cracks a crystal glass!
She sinned, but just enough to let us see
   That God's word must be true, all, sinners be.
So much did zeal her conscience rarefy,
   That, extreme truth lacked little of a lie,
Making omissions, acts; laying the touch
   Of sin, on things that sometimes may be such.

As Moses' cherubins, whose natures do
    Surpass all speed, by him are winged too:
So would her soul, already in heaven, seem then,
    To climb by tears, the common stairs of men.
How fit she was for God, I am content
    To speak, that death his vain haste may repent.
How fit for us, how even and how sweet,
    How good in all her titles, and how meet,
To have reformed this forward heresy,
    That women can no parts of friendship be;
How moral, how divine shall not be told,
    Lest they that hear her virtues, think her old:
And lest we take death's part, and make him glad
    Of such a prey, and to his triumph add.

La Corona

1

Deign at my hands this crown of prayer and praise,
Weaved in my low devout melancholy,
Thou which of good, hast, yea art treasury,
All changing unchanged ancient of days;
But do not, with a vile crown of frail bays,
Reward my muse's white sincerity,
But what thy thorny crown gained, that give me,
A crown of glory, which doth flower always;
The ends crown our works, but thou crown'st our ends,
For, at our end begins our endless rest;
The first last end, now zealously possessed,
With a strong sober thirst, my soul attends.
'Tis time that heart and voice be lifted high,
Salvation to all that will is nigh.

2 ANNUNCIATION

Salvation to all that will is nigh;
That all, which always is all everywhere,
Which cannot sin, and yet all sins must bear,
Which cannot die, yet cannot choose but die,
Lo, faithful Virgin, yields himself to lie
In prison, in thy womb; and though he there
Can take no sin, nor thou give, yet he will wear
Taken from thence, flesh, which death's force may try.
Ere by the spheres time was created, thou
Wast in his mind, who is thy son, and brother;
Whom thou conceiv'st, conceived; yea thou art now
Thy maker's maker, and thy father's mother;
Thou hast light in dark; and shutst in little room,
Immensity cloistered in thy dear womb.

3 NATIVITY

Immensity cloistered in thy dear womb,
Now leaves his well-beloved imprisonment,
There he hath made himself to his intent
Weak enough, now into our world to come;
But oh, for thee, for him, hath th'inn no room?
Yet lay him in this stall, and from the Orient,
Stars, and wisemen will travel to prevent
Th'effect of Herod's jealous general doom.
Seest thou, my soul, with thy faith's eyes, how he
Which fills all place, yet none holds him, doth lie?
Was not his pity towards thee wondrous high,
That would have need to be pitied by thee?
Kiss him, and with him into Egypt go,
With his kind mother, who partakes thy woe.

4 TEMPLE

With his kind mother who partakes thy woe,
Joseph turn back; see where your child doth sit,
Blowing, yea blowing out those sparks of wit,
Which himself on the doctors did bestow;
The Word but lately could not speak, and lo

It suddenly speaks wonders, whence comes it,
That all which was, and all which should be writ,
A shallow seeming child, should deeply know?
His godhead was not soul to his manhood,
Nor had time mellowed him to this ripeness,
But as for one which hath a long task, 'tis good,
With the sun to begin his business,
He in his age's morning thus began
By miracles exceeding power of man.

5   CRUCIFYING

By miracles exceeding power of man,
He faith in some, envy in some begat,
For, what weak spirits admire, ambitious hate;
In both affections many to him ran,
But oh! the worst are most, they will and can,
Alas, and do, unto the immaculate,
Whose creature fate is, now prescribe a fate,
Measuring self-life's infinity to a span,
Nay to an inch. Lo, where condemned he
Bears his own cross, with pain, yet by and by
When it bears him, he must bear more and die.
Now thou art lifted up, draw me to thee,
And at thy death giving such liberal dole,
Moist, with one drop of thy blood, my dry soul.

6   RESURRECTION

Moist, with one drop of thy blood, my dry soul
Shall (though she now be in extreme degree
Too stony hard, and yet too fleshly) be
Freed by that drop, from being starved, hard, or foul,
And life, by this death abled, shall control
Death, whom thy death slew; nor shall to me
Fear of first or last death, bring misery,
If in thy little book my name thou enrol,
Flesh in that long sleep is not putrefied,
But made that there, of which, and for which 'twas;
Nor can by other means be glorified.
May then sin's sleep, and death's soon from me pass,

That waked from both, I again risen may
Salute the last, and everlasting day.

7 ASCENSION

Salute the last and everlasting day,
Joy at the uprising of this sun, and son,
Ye whose just tears, or tribulation
Have purely washed, or burnt your drossy clay;
Behold the Highest, parting hence away,
Lightens the dark clouds, which he treads upon,
Nor doth he by ascending, show alone,
But first he, and he first enters the way.
O strong ram, which hast battered heaven for me,
Mild lamb, which with thy blood, hast marked the path;
Bright torch, which shin'st, that I the way may see,
Oh, with thy own blood quench thy own just wrath,
And if thy holy Spirit, my Muse did raise,
Deign at my hands this crown of prayer and praise.

Holy Sonnets

I Thou hast made me, and shall thy work decay?
   Repair me now, for now mine end doth haste,
   I run to death, and death meets me as fast,
   And all my pleasures are like yesterday;
   I dare not move my dim eyes any way,
   Despair behind, and death before doth cast
   Such terror, and my feeble flesh doth waste
   By sin in it, which it t'wards hell doth weigh;
   Only thou art above, and when towards thee
   By thy leave I can look, I rise again;
   But our old subtle foe so tempteth me,
   That not one hour myself I can sustain;
   Thy grace may wing me to prevent his art,
   And thou like adamant draw mine iron heart.

II As due by many titles I resign
   Myself to thee, O God, first I was made

By thee, and for thee, and when I was decayed
Thy blood bought that, the which before was thine;
I am thy son, made with thyself to shine,
Thy servant, whose pains thou hast still repaid,
Thy sheep, thine image, and, till I betrayed
Myself, a temple of thy Spirit divine;
Why doth the devil then usurp on me?
Why doth he steal, nay ravish that's thy right?
Except thou rise and for thine own work fight,
Oh I shall soon despair, when I do see
That thou lov'st mankind well, yet wilt not choose me,
And Satan hates me, yet is loth to lose me.

III   O might those sighs and tears return again
      Into my breast and eyes, which I have spent,
      That I might in this holy discontent
      Mourn with some fruit, as I have mourned in vain;
      In mine idolatry what showers of rain
      Mine eyes did waste? what griefs my heart did rent?
      That sufferance was my sin; now I repent;
      'Cause I did suffer I must suffer pain.
      Th'hydroptic drunkard, and night-scouting thief,
      The itchy lecher, and self-tickling proud
      Have the remembrance of past joys, for relief
      Of coming ills. To (poor) me is allowed
      No ease; for, long, yet vehement grief hath been
      The effect and cause, the punishment and sin.

IV   Oh my black soul! now thou art summoned
     By sickness, death's herald, and champion;
     Thou art like a pilgrim, which abroad hath done
     Treason, and durst not turn to whence he is fled,
     Or like a thief, which till death's doom be read,
     Wisheth himself delivered from prison;
     But damned and haled to execution,
     Wisheth that still he might be imprisoned.
     Yet grace, if thou repent, thou canst not lack;
     But who shall give thee that grace to begin?
     Oh make thyself with holy mourning black,
     And red with blushing, as thou art with sin;

Or wash thee in Christ's blood, which hath this might
That being red, it dyes red souls to white.

V I am a little world made cunningly
   Of elements, and an angelic sprite,
   But black sin hath betrayed to endless night
   My world's both parts, and (oh) both parts must die.
   You which beyond that heaven which was most high
   Have found new spheres, and of new lands can write,
   Pour new seas in mine eyes, that so I might
   Drown my world with my weeping earnestly,
   Or wash it if it must be drowned no more:
   But oh it must be burnt! alas the fire
   Of lust and envy have burnt it heretofore,
   And made it fouler; let their flames retire,
   And burn me O Lord, with a fiery zeal
   Of thee and thy house, which doth in eating heal.

VI This is my play's last scene, here heavens appoint
    My pilgrimage's last mile; and my race
    Idly, yet quickly run, hath this last pace,
    My span's last inch, my minute's latest point,
    And gluttonous death, will instantly unjoint
    My body, and soul, and I shall sleep a space,
    But my ever-waking part shall see that face,
    Whose fear already shakes my every joint:
    Then, as my soul, to heaven her first seat, takes flight,
    And earth-born body, in the earth shall dwell,
    So, fall my sins, that all may have their right,
    To where they are bred, and would press me, to hell.
    Impute me righteous, thus purged of evil,
    For thus I leave the world, the flesh, the devil.

VII At the round earth's imagined corners, blow
     Your trumpets, angels, and arise, arise
     From death, you numberless infinities
     Of souls, and to your scattered bodies go,
     All whom the flood did, and fire shall o'erthrow,
     All whom war, dearth, age, agues, tyrannies,
     Despair, law, chance, hath slain, and you whose eyes,

Shall behold God, and never taste death's woe.
But let them sleep, Lord, and me mourn a space,
For, if above all these, my sins abound,
'Tis late to ask abundance of thy grace,
When we are there; here on this lowly ground,
Teach me how to repent; for that's as good
As if thou hadst sealed my pardon, with thy blood.

VIII   If faithful souls be alike glorified
As angels, then my father's soul doth see,
And adds this even to full felicity,
That valiantly I hell's wide mouth o'erstride:
But if our minds to these souls be descried
By circumstances, and by signs that be
Apparent in us, not immediately,
How shall my mind's white truth by them be tried?
They see idolatrous lovers weep and mourn,
And vile blasphemous conjurers to call
On Jesus' name, and pharisaical
Dissemblers feign devotion. Then turn
O pensive soul, to God, for he knows best
Thy true grief, for he put it in my breast.

IX   If poisonous minerals, and if that tree,
Whose fruit threw death on else immortal us,
If lecherous goats, if serpents envious
Cannot be damned, alas, why should I be?
Why should intent or reason, born in me,
Make sins, else equal, in me more heinous?
And mercy being easy, and glorious
To God, in his stern wrath, why threatens he?
But who am I, that dare dispute with thee
O God? Oh! of thine only worthy blood,
And my tears, make a heavenly Lethean flood,
And drown in it my sin's black memory;
That thou remember them, some claim as debt,
I think it mercy, if thou wilt forget.

X   Death be not proud, though some have called thee
Mighty and dreadful, for, thou art not so,

For, those, whom thou think'st, thou dost overthrow,
Die not, poor death, nor yet canst thou kill me.
From rest and sleep, which but thy pictures be,
Much pleasure, then from thee, much more must flow,
And soonest our best men with thee do go,
Rest of their bones, and soul's delivery.
Thou art slave to fate, chance, kings, and desperate men,
And dost with poison, war, and sickness dwell,
And poppy, or charms can make us sleep as well,
And better than thy stroke; why swell'st thou then?
One short sleep past, we wake eternally,
And death shall be no more; death, thou shalt die.

XI   Spit in my face you Jews, and pierce my side,
Buffet, and scoff, scourge, and crucify me,
For I have sinned, and sinned, and only he,
Who could do no iniquity, hath died:
But by my death cannot be satisfied
My sins, which pass the Jews' impiety:
They killed once an inglorious man, but I
Crucify him daily, being now glorified.
Oh let me then, his strange love still admire:
Kings pardon, but he bore our punishment.
And Jacob came clothed in vile harsh attire
But to supplant, and with gainful intent:
God clothed himself in vile man's flesh, that so
He might be weak enough to suffer woe.

XII Why are we by all creatures waited on?
Why do the prodigal elements supply
Life and food to me, being more pure than I,
Simple, and further from corruption?
Why brook'st thou, ignorant horse, subjection?
Why dost thou bull, and boar so sillily
Dissemble weakness, and by one man's stroke die,
Whose whole kind, you might swallow and feed upon?
Weaker I am, woe is me, and worse than you,
You have not sinned, nor need be timorous.
But wonder at a greater wonder, for to us
Created nature doth these things subdue,

But their Creator, whom sin, nor nature tied,
For us, his creatures, and his foes, hath died.

XIII What if this present were the world's last night?
Mark in my heart, O soul, where thou dost dwell,
The picture of Christ crucified, and tell
Whether that countenance can thee affright,
Tears in his eyes quench the amazing light,
Blood fills his frowns, which from his pierced head fell.
And can that tongue adjudge thee unto hell,
Which prayed forgiveness for his foes' fierce spite?
No, no; but as in my idolatry
I said to all my profane mistresses,
Beauty, of pity, foulness only is
A sign of rigor: so I say to thee,
To wicked spirits are horrid shapes assigned,
This beauteous form assures a piteous mind.

XIV Batter my heart, three-personed God; for, you
As yet but knock, breathe, shine, and seek to mend;
That I may rise, and stand, o'erthrow me, and bend
Your force, to break, blow, burn and make me new.
I, like an usurped town, to another due,
Labor to admit you, but oh, to no end,
Reason your viceroy in me, me should defend,
But is captived, and proves weak or untrue.
Yet dearly I love you, and would be loved fain,
But am betrothed unto your enemy:
Divorce me, untie, or break that knot again,
Take me to you, imprison me, for I
Except you enthrall me, never shall be free,
Nor ever chaste, except you ravish me.

XV Wilt thou love God, as he thee? then digest,
My soul, this wholesome meditation,
How God the Spirit, by angels waited on
In heaven, doth make his temple in thy breast.
The Father having begot a Son most blessed,
And still begetting, (for he ne'er begun)
Hath deigned to choose thee by adoption,

Coheir to his glory, and Sabbath's endless rest;
And as a robbed man, which by search doth find
His stol'n stuff sold, must lose or buy it again:
The Son of glory came down, and was slain,
Us whom he had made, and Satan stol'n, to unbind.
'Twas much, that man was made like God before,
But, that God should be made like man, much more.

XVI   Father, part of his double interest
     Unto thy kingdom, thy Son gives to me,
     His jointure in the knotty Trinity
     He keeps, and gives to me his death's conquest.
     This Lamb, whose death, with life the world hath blessed,
     Was from the world's beginning slain, and he
     Hath made two wills, which with the Legacy
     Of his and thy kingdom, do thy sons invest.
     Yet such are thy laws, that men argue yet
     Whether a man those statutes can fulfill;
     None doth; but all-healing grace and spirit
     Revive again what law and letter kill.
     Thy law's abridgment, and thy last command
     Is all but love; oh let this last will stand!

XVII   Since she whom I loved hath paid her last debt
     To nature, and to hers, and my good is dead,
     And her soul early into heaven ravished,
     Wholly on heavenly things my mind is set.
     Here the admiring her my mind did whet
     To seek thee God; so streams do show their head;
     But though I have found thee, and thou my thirst hast fed,
     A holy thirsty dropsy melts me yet.
     But why should I beg more love, when as thou
     Dost woo my soul for hers; offering all thine:
     And dost not only fear lest I allow
     My love to saints and angels things divine,
     But in thy tender jealousy dost doubt
     Lest the world, flesh, yea devil put thee out.

XVIII   Show me dear Christ, thy spouse, so bright and clear.
     What! is it she, which on the other shore

Goes richly painted? or which robbed and tore
Laments and mourns in Germany and here?
Sleeps she a thousand, then peeps up one year?
Is she self truth and errs? now new, now outwore?
Doth she, and did she, and shall she evermore
On one, on seven, or on no hill appear?
Dwells she with us, or like adventuring knights
First travail we to seek and then make love?
Betray kind husband thy spouse to our sights,
And let mine amorous soul court thy mild dove,
Who is most true, and pleasing to thee, then
When she is embraced and open to most men.

XIX   Oh, to vex me, contraries meet in one:
Inconstancy unnaturally hath begot
A constant habit; that when I would not
I change in vows, and in devotion.
As humorous is my contrition
As my profane love, and as soon forgot:
As riddlingly distempered, cold and hot,
As praying, as mute; as infinite, as none.
I durst not view heaven yesterday; and today
In prayers, and flattering speeches I court God:
Tomorrow I quake with true fear of his rod.
So my devout fits come and go away
Like a fantastic ague: save that here
Those are my best days, when I shake with fear.

Good Friday, 1613. Riding Westward

Let man's soul be a sphere, and then, in this,
The intelligence that moves, devotion is,
And as the other spheres, by being grown
Subject to foreign motions, lose their own,
And being by others hurried every day,
Scarce in a year their natural form obey:
Pleasure or business, so, our souls admit
For their first mover, and are whirled by it.

Hence is't, that I am carried towards the west
This day, when my soul's form bends toward the east.
There I should see a sun, by rising set,
And by that setting endless day beget;
But that Christ on this Cross, did rise and fall,
Sin had eternally benighted all.
Yet dare I almost be glad, I do not see
That spectacle of too much weight for me.
Who sees God's face, that is self life, must die;
What a death were it then to see God die?
It made his own lieutenant Nature shrink,
It made his footstool crack, and the sun wink.
Could I behold those hands which span the poles,
And tune all spheres at once, pierced with those holes?
Could I behold that endless height which is
Zenith to us, and our antipodes,
Humbled below us? or that blood which is
The seat of all our souls, if not of his,
Made dirt of dust, or that flesh which was worn
By God, for his apparel, ragged, and torn?
If on these things I durst not look, durst I
Upon his miserable mother cast mine eye,
Who was God's partner here, and furnished thus
Half of that sacrifice, which ransomed us?
Though these things, as I ride, be from mine eye,
They are present yet unto my memory,
For that looks towards them; and thou look'st towards me,
O Savior, as thou hang'st upon the tree;
I turn my back to thee, but to receive
Corrections, till thy mercies bid thee leave.
O think me worth thine anger, punish me,
Burn off my rusts, and my deformity,
Restore thine image, so much, by thy grace,
That thou may'st know me, and I'll turn my face.

A Hymn to Christ, at the Author's Last Going into Germany

In what torn ship soever I embark,
That ship shall be my emblem of thy ark;
What sea soever swallow me, that flood
Shall be to me an emblem of thy blood;
Though thou with clouds of anger do disguise
Thy face; yet through that mask I know those eyes,
   Which, though they turn away sometimes,
      They never will despise.

I sacrifice this island unto thee,
And all whom I loved there, and who loved me;
When I have put our seas 'twixt them and me,
Put thou thy sea betwixt my sins and thee.
As the tree's sap doth seek the root below
In winter, in my winter now I go,
   Where none but thee, th'eternal root
      Of true love I may know.

Nor thou nor thy religion dost control,
The amorousness of an harmonious soul,
But thou would'st have that love thyself: as thou
Art jealous, Lord, so I am jealous now,
Thou lov'st not, till from loving more, thou free
My soul: whoever gives, takes liberty:
   O, if thou car'st not whom I love
      Alas, thou lov'st not me.

Seal then this bill of my divorce to all,
On whom those fainter beams of love did fall;
Marry those loves, which in youth scattered be
On fame, wit, hopes (false mistresses) to thee.
Churches are best for prayer, that have least light:
To see God only, I go out of sight:
   And to 'scape stormy days, I choose
      An everlasting night.

Hymn to God My God, in My Sickness

Since I am coming to that holy room,
    Where, with thy choir of saints for evermore,
I shall be made thy music; as I come
    I tune the instrument here at the door,
    And what I must do then, think here before.

Whilst my physicians by their love are grown
    Cosmographers, and I their map, who lie
Flat on this bed, that by them may be shown
    That this is my southwest discovery
    Per fretum febris,[1] by these straits to die,

I joy, that in these straits, I see my west;
    For, though their currents yield return to none,
What shall my west hurt me? As west and east
    In all flat maps (and I am one) are one,
    So death doth touch the resurrection.

Is the Pacific Sea my home? Or are
    The eastern riches? Is Jerusalem?
Anyan, and Magellan, and Gibraltar,
    All straits, and none but straits, are ways to them,
    Whether where Japhet dwelt, or Cham, or Shem.

We think that Paradise and Calvary,
    Christ's Cross, and Adam's tree, stood in one place;
Look Lord, and find both Adams met in me;
    As the first Adam's sweat surrounds my face,
    May the last Adam's blood my soul embrace.

So, in his purple wrapped receive me Lord,
    By these his thorns give me his other crown;
And as to others' souls I preached thy word,
    Be this my text, my sermon to mine own,
    Therefore that he may raise the Lord throws down.

---

[1] Through the strait of fever.

A Hymn to God the Father

Wilt thou forgive that sin where I begun,
　　Which is my sin, though it were done before?
Wilt thou forgive those sins, through which I run,
　　And do run still: though still I do deplore?
　　　　When thou hast done, thou hast not done,
　　　　　　For, I have more.

Wilt thou forgive that sin by which I have won
　　Others to sin? and, made my sin their door?
Wilt thou forgive that sin which I did shun
　　A year, or two: but wallowed in, a score?
　　　　When thou hast done, thou hast not done,
　　　　　　For I have more.

I have a sin of fear, that when I have spun
　　My last thread, I shall perish on the shore;
Swear by thyself, that at my death thy sun
　　Shall shine as he shines now, and heretofore;
　　　　And, having done that, thou hast done,
　　　　　　I fear no more.

Alphabetical List of Titles

Alphabetical List of First Lines

75

DOVER · THRIFT · EDITIONS

All books complete and unabridged. All 5³⁄₁₆″ × 8¼″, paperbound.
Just $1.00–$2.00 in U.S.A.

POETRY

GREAT LOVE POEMS, Shane Weller (ed.). 128pp. 27284-2 $1.00

SELECTED POEMS, Walt Whitman. 128pp. 26878-0 $1.00

THE BALLAD OF READING GAOL AND OTHER POEMS, Oscar Wilde. 64pp. 27072-6 $1.00

FAVORITE POEMS, William Wordsworth. 80pp. 27073-4 $1.00

EARLY POEMS, William Butler Yeats. 128pp. 27808-5 $1.00

FICTION

FLATLAND: A ROMANCE OF MANY DIMENSIONS, Edwin A. Abbott. 96pp. 27263-X $1.00

BEOWULF, Beowulf (trans. by R. K. Gordon). 64pp. 27264-8 $1.00

CIVIL WAR STORIES, Ambrose Bierce. 128pp. 28038-1 $1.00

ALICE'S ADVENTURES IN WONDERLAND, Lewis Carroll. 96pp. 27543-4 $1.00

O PIONEERS!, Willa Cather. 128pp. 27785-2 $1.00

FIVE GREAT SHORT STORIES, Anton Chekhov. 96pp. 26463-7 $1.00

FAVORITE FATHER BROWN STORIES, G. K. Chesterton. 96pp. 27545-0 $1.00

THE AWAKENING, Kate Chopin. 128pp. 27786-0 $1.00

HEART OF DARKNESS, Joseph Conrad. 80pp. 26464-5 $1.00

THE SECRET SHARER AND OTHER STORIES, Joseph Conrad. 128pp. 27546-9 $1.00

THE OPEN BOAT AND OTHER STORIES, Stephen Crane. 128pp. 27547-7 $1.00

THE RED BADGE OF COURAGE, Stephen Crane. 112pp. 26465-3 $1.00

A CHRISTMAS CAROL, Charles Dickens. 80pp. 26865-9 $1.00

THE CRICKET ON THE HEARTH AND OTHER CHRISTMAS STORIES, Charles Dickens. 128pp. 28039-X $1.00

NOTES FROM THE UNDERGROUND, Fyodor Dostoyevsky. 96pp. 27053-X $1.00

SIX GREAT SHERLOCK HOLMES STORIES, Sir Arthur Conan Doyle. 112pp. 27055-6 $1.00

WHERE ANGELS FEAR TO TREAD, E. M. Forster. 128pp. (Available in U.S. only) 27791-7 $1.00

THE OVERCOAT AND OTHER SHORT STORIES, Nikolai Gogol. 112pp. 27057-2 $1.00

GREAT GHOST STORIES, John Grafton (ed.). 112pp. 27270-2 $1.00

THE LUCK OF ROARING CAMP AND OTHER SHORT STORIES, Bret Harte. 96pp. 27271-0 $1.00

THE SCARLET LETTER, Nathaniel Hawthorne. 192pp. 28048-9 $2.00

YOUNG GOODMAN BROWN AND OTHER SHORT STORIES, Nathaniel Hawthorne. 128pp. 27060-2 $1.00

THE GIFT OF THE MAGI AND OTHER SHORT STORIES, O. Henry. 96pp. 27061-0 $1.00

THE NUTCRACKER AND THE GOLDEN POT, E. T. A. Hoffmann. 128pp. 27806-9 $1.00

THE BEAST IN THE JUNGLE AND OTHER STORIES, Henry James. 128pp. 27552-3 $1.00

THE TURN OF THE SCREW, Henry James. 96pp. 26684-2 $1.00

DUBLINERS, James Joyce. 160pp. 26870-5 $1.00

A PORTRAIT OF THE ARTIST AS A YOUNG MAN, James Joyce. 192pp. 28050-0 $2.00

DOVER · THRIFT · EDITIONS

All books complete and unabridged. All 5³⁄₁₆″ × 8¼″, paperbound.
Just $1.00–$2.00 in U.S.A.

FICTION

THE MAN WHO WOULD BE KING AND OTHER STORIES, Rudyard Kipling. 128pp. 28051-9 $1.00

SELECTED SHORT STORIES, D. H. Lawrence. 128pp. 27794-1 $1.00

GREEN TEA AND OTHER GHOST STORIES, J. Sheridan LeFanu. 96pp. 27795-X $1.00

THE CALL OF THE WILD, Jack London. 64pp. 26472-6 $1.00

FIVE GREAT SHORT STORIES, Jack London. 96pp. 27063-7 $1.00

WHITE FANG, Jack London. 160pp. 26968-X $1.00

THE NECKLACE AND OTHER SHORT STORIES, Guy de Maupassant. 128pp. 27064-5 $1.00

BARTLEBY AND BENITO CERENO, Herman Melville. 112pp. 26473-4 $1.00

THE GOLD-BUG AND OTHER TALES, Edgar Allan Poe. 128pp. 26875-6 $1.00

THE QUEEN OF SPADES AND OTHER STORIES, Alexander Pushkin. 128pp. 28054-3 $1.00

THREE LIVES, Gertrude Stein. 176pp. 28059-4 $2.00

THE STRANGE CASE OF DR. JEKYLL AND MR. HYDE, Robert Louis Stevenson. 64pp. 26688-5 $1.00

TREASURE ISLAND, Robert Louis Stevenson. 160pp. 27559-0 $1.00

THE KREUTZER SONATA AND OTHER SHORT STORIES, Leo Tolstoy. 144pp. 27805-0 $1.00

ADVENTURES OF HUCKLEBERRY FINN, Mark Twain. 224pp. 28061-6 $2.00

THE MYSTERIOUS STRANGER AND OTHER STORIES, Mark Twain. 128pp. 27069-6 $1.00

CANDIDE, Voltaire (François-Marie Arouet). 112pp. 26689-3 $1.00

THE INVISIBLE MAN, H. G. Wells. 112pp. (Available in U.S. only.) 27071-8 $1.00

ETHAN FROME, Edith Wharton. 96pp. 26690-7 $1.00

THE PICTURE OF DORIAN GRAY, Oscar Wilde. 192pp. 27807-7 $1.00

NONFICTION

THE DEVIL'S DICTIONARY, Ambrose Bierce. 144pp. 27542-6 $1.00

THE SOULS OF BLACK FOLK, W. E. B. Du Bois. 176pp. 28041-1 $2.00

SELF-RELIANCE AND OTHER ESSAYS, Ralph Waldo Emerson. 128pp. 27790-9 $1.00

GREAT SPEECHES, Abraham Lincoln. 112pp. 26872-1 $1.00

THE PRINCE, Niccolò Machiavelli. 80pp. 27274-5 $1.00

SYMPOSIUM AND PHAEDRUS, Plato. 96pp. 27798-4 $1.00

THE TRIAL AND DEATH OF SOCRATES: FOUR DIALOGUES, Plato. 128pp. 27066-1 $1.00

CIVIL DISOBEDIENCE AND OTHER ESSAYS, Henry David Thoreau. 96pp. 27563-9 $1.00

THE THEORY OF THE LEISURE CLASS, Thorstein Veblen. 256pp. 28062-4 $2.00

PLAYS

THE CHERRY ORCHARD, Anton Chekhov. 64pp. 26682-6 $1.00

THE THREE SISTERS, Anton Chekhov. 64pp. 27544-2 $1.00

THE WAY OF THE WORLD, William Congreve. 80pp. 27787-9 $1.00

MEDEA, Euripides. 64pp. 27548-5 $1.00

THE MIKADO, William Schwenck Gilbert. 64pp. 27268-0 $1.00

DOVER · THRIFT · EDITIONS

All books complete and unabridged. All 5³⁄₁₆″ × 8¼″, paperbound.
Just $1.00–$2.00 in U.S.A.

PLAYS

FAUST, PART ONE, Johann Wolfgang von Goethe. 192pp. 28046-2 $2.00

SHE STOOPS TO CONQUER, Oliver Goldsmith. 80pp. 26867-5 $1.00

A DOLL'S HOUSE, Henrik Ibsen. 80pp. 27062-9 $1.00

HEDDA GABLER, Henrik Ibsen. 80pp. 26469-6 $1.00

VOLPONE, Ben Jonson. 112pp. 28049-7 $1.00

THE MISANTHROPE, Molière. 64pp. 27065-3 $1.00

HAMLET, William Shakespeare. 128pp. 27278-8 $1.00

JULIUS CAESAR, William Shakespeare. 80pp. 26876-4 $1.00

KING LEAR, William Shakespeare. 112pp. 28058-6 $1.00

MACBETH, William Shakespeare. 96pp. 27802-6 $1.00

A MIDSUMMER NIGHT'S DREAM, William Shakespeare. 80pp. 27067-X $1.00

ROMEO AND JULIET, William Shakespeare. 96pp. 27557-4 $1.00

ARMS AND THE MAN, George Bernard Shaw. 80pp. (Available in U.S. only.) 26476-9 $1.00

THE SCHOOL FOR SCANDAL, Richard Brinsley Sheridan. 96pp. 26687-7 $1.00

ANTIGONE, Sophocles. 64pp. 27804-2 $1.00

OEDIPUS REX, Sophocles. 64pp. 26877-2 $1.00

MISS JULIE, August Strindberg. 64pp. 27281-8 $1.00

THE PLAYBOY OF THE WESTERN WORLD AND RIDERS TO THE SEA, J. M. Synge. 80pp. 27562-0 $1.00

THE IMPORTANCE OF BEING EARNEST, Oscar Wilde. 64pp. 26478-5 $1.00

For a complete descriptive list of all volumes in the Dover Thrift Editions series
write for a free Dover Fiction and Literature Catalog (59047-X) to
Dover Publications, Inc., Dept. DTE, 31 E. 2nd Street, Mineola, NY 11501